Women as Entrepreneurs

Women as Entrepreneurs:

A Study of Female Business Owners, Their Motivations,
Experiences and Strategies for Success

SARA CARTER
Scottish Enterprise Foundation
University of Stirling

TOM CANNON
Manchester Business School

HD
2346
.G7
W65X
1992
West

ACADEMIC PRESS
Harcourt Brace Jovanovich, Publishers
London   San Diego   New York   Boston
Sydney   Tokyo   Toronto

ACADEMIC PRESS LIMITED
24–28 Oval Road
London NW1 7DX

US edition published by
ACADEMIC PRESS INC
San Diego, CA 92101

ISBN 0-12-161755-6

Typeset by Paston Press, Loddon, Norfolk
Printed and bound in Great Britain by TJ Press, Padstow, Cornwall

Contents

Contents

Preface

The last decade has witnessed a rapid increase in the number of women starting their own business, both in Britain and abroad. The surge in entrepreneurial activity between 1981 and 1987 saw male self-employment increase by 30%, but at the same time female self-employment increased by 70%. Women now account for one-quarter of the self-employed in Britain. This increase has been mirrored in other Western countries throughout the 1980s and looks likely to continue into the 1990s. While much has been published on the subject of self-employment and small business ownership from a number of different perspectives, most has concentrated upon the male-owned enterprise. The role of women as owner-managers and employers has been largely neglected as an area of serious academic study, despite the fact that greater numbers of women are now choosing self-employment.

As a response to this situation, the Department of Employment and Shell (UK) Ltd commissioned a team of researchers at the Scottish Enterprise Foundation, University of Stirling, to undertake a study into female entrepreneurship. The study was to investigate the reasons why women start in business, the problems (gender and non-gender related) that they faced and the strategies successful women adopted to overcome barriers. The research team took a case study approach to the investigation. Sixty female entrepreneurs from a variety of different industrial sectors were interviewed. The women varied in many ways: their ages; their experience of management and self-employment; the size of business they owned; the number of people they employed; even whether they had started businesses with partners or by themselves. A parallel study was conducted of 10 women who had been in business, but who had subsequently ceased trading. This was used to give an alternative perspective on the issues involved. This group gave the research team an insight into the causes of and attitudes towards 'failure' of women. If few studies have been undertaken looking at the successful female entrepreneur, fewer still have addressed the causes and consequences of business failure by women. This study was in part, at least, an attempt to redress this lack of knowledge.

A picture emerged of a growing number of entrepreneurs who share some common features, but who have significantly different experiences than their male counterparts. Differences in motivations for start up, the problems they experience and most importantly, their attitudes towards 'success' and 'failure' distinguish female business owners and starters as a group worthy of attention in their own right. This book is based upon the findings of that study.

The definition of the terms 'entrepreneurship' and 'small business' has preoccupied scholars over several years, without any satisfactory level of agreement. For the purposes of this study a flexible interpretation was assumed. Here the terms include women in a wide variety of industrial sectors, using different forms of ownership structure, and with contrasting personal experience. In each case, however, the respondent took the lead in the establishment and organization of her particular enterprise. While some co-operatives and partnerships (eight co-owned by husbands or domestic partners) were included in the study, these were only included after it had been established that the female respondent had initiated the enterprise and was involved, at ownership level, in the day-to-day management of the business.

The need to conduct studies specifically into women's business ownership is based on the proposition that women face problems some of which are in addition to, or different from, those met by men, in starting and running businesses. The management of domestic commitments and childcare support are two issues which have an obvious gender dimension for all working women. Other, generic business issues, such as raising finance and finding clients, common to all small business owners, have a less obvious gender relationship. These may prove more difficult to overcome. Despite these problems, a significant number of women have created successful businesses. These women may not be owner-managers of multinational enterprises or directors of public companies. They are ordinary women who have started their own small business. In doing so, however, many have had to confront an array of problems. As a method of resolving these difficulties, many developed strategies, either as a conscious or subconscious approach, to overcome barriers. Often strategies were adopted as early as the pre-start-up phase and determined the way respondents planned for self-employment. Some women gained management experience and financial backing. Others developed business skills and involved themselves in local business networks. Many developed distinctive approaches. Market selection often emerged as part of a strategy for self-employment. Respondents showed remarkable similarities in the kinds of strategies that they had adopted to deal with specific issues. The case studies presented at the end of each chapter throughout the book illustrate the histories of the women interviewed and the problems they faced in starting and building businesses. Their successful strategies in overcoming problems have implications for all women starting in business.

This book presents the findings of this study. The first chapter provides an analysis of the position of women in the economy, reasons for the rise in the number of female business owners throughout the world and documents previous research into the area. Chapters 2 and 3 introduce the women who participated in the study and review their motivations and experience of starting in business. Chapters 4 and 5 examine the day-to-day lives of women in business, their problems, management styles and strategies for success. The following two chapters examine definitions of and attitudes towards success and failure. The effect of family support on female business ownership is given in Chapter 8. The final chapter concludes the study and presents the recommendations drawn from the findings.

The authors would like to acknowledge the assistance and help they received from a number of sources. Firstly, we would like to thank the Department of Employment and Shell (UK) Ltd for sponsoring this study. In particular, George Clark and Nitya Banerji of the Department of Employment and Jonathan Keene and Asif Abdullah of Shell (UK) Ltd provided invaluable assistance and continuing support throughout the whole project. Researchers Peter Rosa, Lesley Baddon and Rosemary McClure of the Scottish Enterprise Foundation made a significant contribution and provided expertise in interviewing and data analysis. Marilou Cunningham, Brenda Emslie, Sheila Hutton and Kirsty McColl of the Scottish Enterprise Foundation helped to prepare the manuscript. Last, but not least, 70 women from London, Nottinghamshire and Glasgow gave their time generously and unfailingly and, by doing so, they enabled us to conduct this study.

SARA CARTER
TOM CANNON

To Sean, Roisin and Ben
and to Cathy, Vera and Shelagh

1

Introduction

The small business sector has expanded in recent decades stimulated by changes in the industrial structure of Britain and government commitment to encourage new forms of economic enterprise. Throughout the 1980s there was an increase in confidence in the potential of small firms to contribute to the regeneration of the British economy (Williams, 1985). Small firms are now regarded as a vital element in the attempt to increase the rate of job creation, improve competitiveness and exploit new technologies. These benefits require new social attitudes towards enterprise and entrepreneurship (Weiner, 1981). A rise in the rate of small firm formation in the first half of the decade (Ganguly and Bannock, 1985) was sustained in the different economic conditions of recent years. In 1989, new businesses were being established at a net rate of around 1400 per week. Britain now has a larger proportion of self-employment than at any time since the 1920s, accounting for one-tenth of the working population (Curran, 1986).

Increased interest in the small firm sector led to an associated growth of research into small business and the nature of entrepreneurship (London Business School, 1983; Curran, 1986; Cannon et al., 1989). Many significant studies have been undertaken looking at small firms from economic, business and sociological perspectives. The bulk of the work to date has concentrated upon the male-owned enterprise. Research into female entrepreneurship and the role of women as owner managers and employers has been largely neglected as an area of study (Goffee and Scase, 1985) despite the greater numbers of women now choosing self-employment (Curran, 1986).

There has been a sustained rise in the number of women starting businesses in the United Kingdom and elsewhere (Van der Wees and Romijn, 1987). The United States Small Business Administration reported in 1985 that over the previous decade the number of female business owners grew by 74%; women now account for 37% of all new enterprises. The 1988 President's report indicated that this pattern of growth

1

continued during the 1980s. Accordingly, business receipts from women-owned businesses increased from $44 billion to $53 billion in 1983 alone. Similar trends in the growth of female entrepreneurship have been reported in other countries (Van der Wees and Romijn, 1987). Women still, however, represent only a minority of entrepreneurs in proportions varying from one country to another.

In the UK, recent estimates of the number of self-employed men and women display a 'sharply upward trend which has accelerated in the 1980s' (Curran, 1986, p. 3). Between 1981 and 1987, male self-employment increased by 30% but the number of self-employed women increased by 70% (Department of Employment, 1988). Women now account for 25% of all self-employed. This statistic masks the fact that women account for only 16% of all full-time, but more than 70% of all part-time self-employed.

The rise in the number of female self-employed and owner-managers parallels the increasing participation of women, in particular married women, in the labour market. Since 1977, the female share of employment has risen in all occupational groups, with the exception of operatives and labourers (Equal Opportunities Commission, 1989). In 1987, over 9 million women were employed in Britain; 5.1 million in full-time jobs and 4.2 million in part-time jobs (Labour Force Survey, 1987). Table 1.1 gives a breakdown of men and women in employment. Women now make up more than 40% of the entire labour force (Department of Employment, 1988). Scholars working within the area of women's studies have provided a great deal of data and analysis regarding the state of contemporary women's employment in Britain (cf. Hakim, 1979; West, 1982; Martin and Roberts, 1984; Dex, 1987). There is now much evidence to suggest that not only do women work overwhelmingly within a narrow range of industrial sectors and within specific occupational groupings within these sectors, but that their working lives differ substantially to their male counterparts.

Labour market segmentation on the basis of skill, social class, ethnicity and age led many scholars to conclude that there is a 'dual labour market', made up of primary and secondary sectors. Barron and Norris (1976) define a dual labour market as having distinctive characteristics. Within a dual labour market there is a division into high (primary) and low (secondary) paying sectors with restricted mobility between these sectors. Only the high paying sectors offer career or promotional opportunities and occupational security. The primary sector of the labour market is made up of well-paid, secure jobs offering career opportunities and a multitude of fringe benefits to its employees. By contrast, the secondary sector is characterized by low-paid, insecure occupations offering poor working conditions.

Table 1.1 Employment status of people in employment.

	All		Men		Married women		Non-married women*	
	$\times 10^3$	%	$\times 10^3$	%	$\times 10^3$	%	$\times 10^3$	%
All in employment	24 257	100	13 958	100	6 981	100	3 318	100
Employees	20 764	85.6	11 405	81.7	6 347	90.9	3 013	90.8
Full-time†	16 043	66.1	10 904	78.1	2 874	41.2	226	668.3
Part-time	4 708	19.4	495	3.5	3 469	49.7	744	22.4
Self-employed	2 995	12.3	2 233	16.0	616	8.8	146	4.4
Full-time	2 476	10.2	2 081	14.9	298	4.3	96	2.9
Part-time	517	2.1	151	1.1	317	4.5	49	1.5
Employees and self-employed	23 767	98.0	13 644	97.8	6 963	99.7	3 160	95.2
Full-time	18 519	76.3	12 985	93.0	3 172	45.4	2 362	71.2
Part-time	5 225	21.5	646	4.6	3 786	54.2	793	23.9
Gov't employment and training schemes	490	2.0	314	2.2	18	0.3	158	4.8

* Single, widowed, divorced, legally separated.
† Definition of full time or part time is based on the respondent's own assessment, not on the number of hours worked.

Source: 1987 Labour Force Survey, Preliminary Results, *Employment Gazette*, March 1988.

Barron and Norris (1976) state that there are five main attributes that make a particular social group likely candidates for secondary sector workers: dispensability; clearly visible social difference; little interest in acquiring training; low economism; and lack of solidarity. They go on to argue that there are sexual divisions within the dual labour market and that, as a group, women generally fulfil the characteristics of secondary sector workers. They conclude that:

women are the main secondary workforce in Britain, and the fact that the primary–secondary division coincides with sexual divisions in the labour market has obscured the existence of dualism in the British labour market.

Research on labour market segmentation has indicated that there are sexual divisions in the occupational distribution of the work force. Within specific occupational sectors, women often hold the lower paid positions. Further research into patterns of industrial distribution also demonstrates that women are likely to be concentrated into particular sectors of the economy, for example, retail and service sectors.

Table 1.2 shows the industrial sectors of the economy by gender participation. In almost every sector the level of participation by women has increased. The table does not, however, display the occupational segmentation of women into lower paid jobs. The majority of senior positions within most sectors are occupied by men. For example, in banking less than 1% of the branch managers are female and, in retail sales only 26% of managers are female (Oakley, 1982).

Hakim (1979) suggested that the employment life cycle of women can be split into two phases. The first spans employment prior to the birth of a woman's first child. The second phase comes after the youngest child is of school age. A later study (Martin and Roberts, 1984) which collected detailed work histories, suggests that this aggregate bimodal profile masks the fact that for many women the situation is more complex. Women with children often have a more continuous working life, with spells of paid work between children and an earlier return to work after the youngest child reaches school age. Women now spend more of their potential working lives in paid employment, and the trend is towards even greater participation.

Table 1.2   Industrial distribution of male and female employees in Britain, 1981 and 1988.

	Percentages			
	1981		1988	
Industrial sector	Men	Women	Men	Women
Mining and quarrying	95	5	76	24
Construction	92	8	88	12
Vehicles	89	11	87	13
Mechanical engineering	85	15	84	16
Transport communication	81	19	79	21
Paper/printing and publishing	69	31	64	36
Food, drink, tobacco	61	39	58	42
Public administration	58	42	55	45
Textiles	55	45	27	73
Insurance, banking, finance and business services	49	51	50	50
Distributive and retail trade	47	53	36	64
Miscellaneous services	47	53	26	74
Professional and scientific	31	69	—	—
Clothing and footwear	26	74	20	80

Source: New Earnings Survey (1982), *Department of Employment and Employment Gazette*, January 1989.

Despite this increase in both in the number of women in the labour force and in the continuity of their working lives, the position of women in the labour market has remained largely unchanged since the immediate post-war years (Barron and Norris, 1976; Amsden 1980; Bruegel, 1982). Most women still hold low-paid, unskilled or semi-skilled positions. Employment is often part-time, and concentrated in the service sectors. In 1965, only 5% of all working women were managers or employers. This figure was unchanged fifteen years later (Martin and Roberts, 1984). In 1965 the largest concentration of working women was within the category of junior non-manual workers at 39%. In 1980 this group was still the largest, accounting for 36% of all working women. Additionally, distinctions between male and female earnings levels led to a bimodal profile of national earnings distribution patterns (Chiplin and Sloane, 1974, 1982).

British researchers are keen to emphasize the connections between female self-employment and the broader position of women in the labour market. It is argued that self-employment is both a reaction to, and a means of escaping, the persistent segregation and occupational confines of the labour market (Goffee and Scase, 1985; Cromie and Hayes, 1988). Thus, the rise in the number of the female self-employed and owner-managers can be seen to parallel the increasing participation, and the largely unchanging position, of women in the wider labour market.

In their study on female entrepreneurship, Goffee and Scase (1985) make just such a point:

> Setting up a small business . . . can represent an explicit rejection of the exploitative nature of the capitalist work process and labour market. In this sense, then, business proprietorship may be seen as a radical—albeit short-term and individualistic—response to subordination. . . . Thus, women who both own and manage business enterprises—especially those in male-dominated sectors—serve to undermine conventional and stereotyped notions of 'a woman's place'. Female entrepreneurs such as these, therefore, have a symbolic importance which explicitly questions popular conceptions of the position of women in society. Finally, proprietorship can enable women to enjoy some material independence and, in many circumstances, the opportunity to control the products of their own labour (p. 37).

Notwithstanding this, the patterns of industrial distribution among the employed population are largely repeated among the self-employed, with women concentrated in the retail and service sectors. Results of the Labour Force Surveys 1981–1984 indicate that two industrial sectors account for the bulk of all female self-employed (Creigh *et al.*, 1986). The largest sector, 'Distribution, Hotels and Catering', accounts for 41.8% of female self-employment. 'Other Services' accounts for a further 30.5% of female self-employment and 10% of male self-employment. Men are more likely to enter into self-employment in the construction industries (26.5%), the third largest category, than women (1.4%). One in ten of all male employees work in the construction industry compared with only 1.6% of female employees. This illustrates the similarity in bias towards service sectors and away from sectors such as construction, in both female employment and self-employment patterns.

The lack of a national data base on female self-employment limits our knowledge of women in business and makes the construction of representative samples impossible. In Britain, the annual Labour Force Surveys provide the most important source of statistical information regarding the numbers and status of female entrepreneurs. The problems of data collection caused by a lack of detailed statistical information are repeated throughout the world (Van der Wees and Romijn, 1987). Most of the influential studies of women owner-managers have used small samples constructed according to the particular interests of the researchers (Curran, 1986). Goffee and Scase (1985), for example, employed a sample of 54 women ". . . from home-based, self-employed proprietors to owner-managers of international enterprises" (p. 39). The largest, but again non-representative, survey of female entrepreneurs was conducted by the EEC across 10 Member States (Marokjovic, 1987). This study estimated that 13 million women are involved in business ownership, of which 5 million either own their own business or are self-employed, and the remainder work within family businesses, either with or for husbands or parents. The study concluded that most women in business for themselves trade in a small number of industrial sectors, mirroring the findings of the British Labour Force Surveys. Of the 17 000 women questioned in this study, 46% worked in retail sectors, 12% in beauty and health care, 10% in the 'liberal professions'; 9% in agriculture; 9% in handicrafts and only 1% in industry. The study found that women working within agriculture were usually older, less-educated, started working very young and had the lowest average revenue.

The problems caused by the lack of a detailed, nationally representative, quantitative data base should not be underestimated. Despite increasing attention and the advances made in our understanding of the issues involved, certain aspects of the research techniques used and the current research agenda have impeded further progress. The dominance of qualitative methodologies and the absence of nationally collected data, are seen as major stumbling blocks to replicable and verifiable studies. Research into women in business is largely dependent on qualitative data collection techniques, usually involving face-to-face interviews with selected entrepreneurs. Samples have usually been small scale, typically less than 50 respondents. Extrapolation from qualitative research to describe a national phenomenon is highly suspect. Researchers face certain methodological problems when relying on verbal reports and individual explanations to investigate prior or current experiences. Two problems brought about by this type of approach are of immediate importance. First, there are problems concerning the accuracy of retrospective recall of the respondents. Second, there are—especially in the case of small business-related research—also difficulties in distinguishing 'perceived problems' from 'real problems'.

Gender-based research is no exception. The social and political backgrounds of the interviewees often determine whether discrimination is perceived and recognized as such. In other instances the interview itself may be a determining factor. Probing and encouraging the interviewee to discuss her experiences in terms of gender may raise the level of consciousness and recognition of gender discrimination among the respondents. Recognition of discrimination by respondents is generally a function of two particular factors. First, the general awareness of the constraints on labour force participation of women in the overall economy and second, direct experience of gender discrimination as a self-employed woman. Although impossible to isolate and address quantitatively, the issue of perception versus reality is central to many of the findings of studies of female entrepreneurship, particularly in the attribution of certain business problems to gender-related barriers. This can be seen as a direct function of the use of qualitative research techniques. Researchers have, however, demonstrated that it is exceptionally difficult to extract experiences of gender discrimination via the use of quantitative techniques.

Despite these methodological caveats, existing studies into female entrepreneurship have been relatively consistent in their findings and have provided valuable insights into the experiences of women in business. Many of these could not have been achieved solely by a quantitatively based approach. These findings suggest that women often have different motivations for starting in business than men. They have to overcome distinctive problems, often gender related, before starting in business and once trading, they face problems which may inhibit company growth.

Generally, there is more interest and research into the nature and experience of the female entrepreneur in North America than in Britain. This work is influenced by the existing small business and entrepreneurship literature; here 'entrepreneur' is often used as a synonym for owner-manager. Early studies into the area concentrated mainly upon the motivations for business start-up (Schreier, 1975; Schwartz, 1976;

Hisrich and Brush, 1983; Goffee and Scase, 1985), their personality characteristics (Lavoie, 1987) and the gender-related barriers perceived or experienced during this phase of business ownership (Hisrich and Brush, 1983; Watkins and Watkins, 1984; Carter and Cannon, 1988b). Much of the research tried to establish the extent to which women comply with a pattern of entrepreneurial behaviour established with male subjects. Few of the studies developed taxonomies of female entrepreneurs, preferring to identify female proprietors as an homogeneous group, and there has been an implicit assumption by researchers that—beyond the start-up phase—few significant differences exist between male and female owned and managed companies. Thus, scholars of small business have noted that our cumulative knowledge of female entrepreneurship remains limited (Curran, 1986a; Stevenson, 1986), lacks utility and/or rigour (Solomon and Fernald, 1988; Allen and Truman, 1988) and presents a static and therefore distorted view of the process of female business ownership (Carter and Cannon, 1988).

Schreier's (1975) study of female entrepreneurs demonstrated that the female entrepreneur has much in common with her male counterpart, with the exception of the industrial sectors in which women tend to trade. Businesses owned by women tended to reflect traditional female employment in the labour market, mainly in the service sectors. Schwartz (1976) also found a predominance of service-based businesses. Schwartz concluded that female motivations for business start-up were similar to those of men. That is, the search for independence and the challenge of business ownership. The greatest barriers to their business success were financial discrimination, lack of training and business knowledge and underestimating the cost of sustaining a business.

More recent American research examines in greater depth both the motivations for female business start-up and the problems faced by women when starting a business (Hisrich and Brush, 1983). Motivations for business start-up were identified as a desire for job satisfaction, independence and achievement. These are described as being largely unattainable in the formal labour market. The major problems, identified by the female respondents in this study, were under-capitalization and a lack of knowledge and training in business skills. A majority of the respondents reported difficulties in "overcoming some of the social beliefs that women are not as serious as men about business". Hisrich and Brush (1986) found evidence of contrasting experience of women operating in different sectors. Women in non-traditionally female sectors (that is, those dominated by male employees, such as construction and manufacturing industries) experienced more problems in raising finance. In both non-traditional and new sectors, female business owners were hampered by their lack of business training. Hisrich and Brush concluded that barriers experienced by female entrepreneurs often relate to the sectors in which they trade. A later study (Hisrich and Brush, 1986) focused on different types of female-owned business and confirmed the lack of support offered to female proprietors in non-traditional sectors.

In Britain, studies investigating female entrepreneurship are scarce in comparison with the volume of work undertaken in the area of small business and entrepreneurship. Curran (1986) states: "to date there have been only two influential (British) studies (Watkins and Watkins, 1984 and Goffee and Scase, 1985) plus a more recent study of female aspiring small business owners (Cromie, 1984)".

Watkins and Watkins (1984) found that the backgrounds and experiences of their sample of 58 female and 43 male business owners differed significantly. Men are more likely to have work experience relevant to their new venture; self-employment provides them with an essentially similar occupation with the added attraction of autonomy. This study also found that most women are unprepared for business start-up, especially within non-traditional sectors. As a consequence they take greater risks than their male counterparts. Watkins and Watkins concluded that the narrow range of prior experience affects the choice of sectors in which women are capable of establishing viable businesses. It forces them into traditionally female sectors. Choice of business sector for women is determined by consideration of which areas posed the fewer obstacles to their success. These were perceived to be those where technical and financial barriers to business entry were low and where managerial proficiency was not considered to be an essential prerequisite to success. As Watkins and Watkins emphasized:

> ... the choice of business can be seen in terms of high motivation to immediate independence tempered by economic rationality, rather than a conscious desire to operate 'female-type' businesses (p. 230).

This risk avoidance policy contrasts with the maximizing opportunity policy of comparable male entrepreneurs.

In a more recent study Goffee and Scase (1985) use a sample of 54 female proprietors to identify a typology of female entrepreneurs. This is based on two factors. First, there is their attachment to conventional entrepreneurial (Smilesean derived) ideals in the form of individualism and self-reliance. Second there is the willingness of the female entrepreneur to accept conventional gender roles, often subordinate to men. Four types of female entrepreneur were identified; 'conventional' entrepreneurs who were highly committed to both entrepreneurial ideals and conventional gender roles; 'innovative' entrepreneurs, who held a strong belief in entrepreneurial ideals but had a relatively low attachment to conventional gender-defined roles; 'domestic' entrepreneurs who organized their life around the family situation and believed very strongly in conventional female roles and held low attachment to entrepreneurial ideals; 'radical' entrepreneurs who held low attachment to both, often organizing their business on a political collectivist basis. A similar, although independently derived, profile of the female entrepreneur was described by Cromie and Hayes (1988) using a sample drawn from Northern Ireland.

The construction of this typology has been criticized by two subsequent studies (Allen and Truman, 1988; Carter and Cannon, 1988b). Allen and Truman argue that the two factors upon which the typology is based, that is, entrepreneurial ideals and adherence to conventional gender roles, are not appropriate for the analysis of female entrepreneurial behaviour.

Allen and Truman state that the socio-economic reality of women's lives means that the majority have very little choice over how attached they can be to 'entrepreneurial ideals'.

> For example, self-help and personal responsibility and reliance has different connotations in different contexts. A single parent trying to earn an income for her family may indeed demonstrate entrepreneurial ideals but the outcome of her entrepreneurship would be quite different from that of a single, childless, male entrepreneur (p. 9).

Allen and Truman's criticism of the second factor identified by Goffee and Scase, "conventionally defined gender roles or the extent to which women accept their subordination to men", centres around the fact that:

> An immediate problem with this approach is that it implies an homogenous experience of women's subordination by men. There is ample evidence in published literature to suggest that female subordination differs in relation to social class, ethnic origin, marital status as well as numerous other factors, both structural and personal (p. 9).

Carter and Cannon (1988b) acknowledge that the Goffee and Scase typology highlights the heterogeneity among female entrepreneurs. Despite this, it underestimates two important features of business ownership. The sector is inherently turbulent. Ventures are started, grow, decline, face change and develop. This ferment calls for many and varying behaviours and attitudes among entrepreneurs. Static descriptors or types will distort reality. Not only are entrepreneurial firms either new, growing or in some state of flux (Begley and Boyd, 1987), but the process of entrepreneurship itself is dynamic and ever-changing (Carsrud, 1988). Until recently, however, change was normally associated with and attributed to various external economic and market-making factors (Schumpeter, 1934, 1943; Kirzner, 1973); as opposed to the internal personal goals and life situations of the individual entrepreneur. *Prima facie* evidence from studies of female entrepreneurs suggests that their personal goals and value profiles may differ significantly from their male counterparts (Allen and Truman, 1988; Solomon and Fernald, 1988). Yet, this assumes a static homogeneity among women which simply does not exist. Thus, the Goffee and Scase typology presents a distorted picture of female entrepreneurship, whereas business ownership, especially in the small firms sector, is a dynamic and often turbulent process: businesses expand, contract, and diversify.

Some owner-managers may seek to stabilize their businesses, but firms rarely exist in the same form for long. Vast diversity exists within these limits of the small firm. Cottage industries can become stable thriving firms. Self-employed designers can become manufacturers. Manufacturers can diversify to produce specialized products.

The typology underestimates the effect business ownership has on the individual entrepreneur, many of whom are changed as a result of the entrepreneurial experience. Thus, the domestics, as defined by Goffee and Scase, may—by the experience of business ownership—become dedicated business owners with a very strong attachment to entrepreneurial ideals. Women who would be defined as 'conventionals', having built up their business and delegated the management, can concentrate on their personal family life and convert to 'domestics'.

Despite the limitations, the work undertaken by Goffee and Scase represents one of the main reference points in our understanding of female entrepreneurship in Britain. The study described in this book was undertaken between 1987 and 1989. The remit was to document the motivations and experiences of women in business in Britain. The task set is to establish not only why, but also how they had started in business, the problems that they had experienced and most important, the strategies adopted by those who succeeded. An understanding of the latter can provide vital insights for future policy of action. Case studies of 60 female entrepreneurs were compiled during a 10-month period up to April 1988. An in-depth, semi-structured questionnaire was used to elicit quantitative data. Open-ended and non-directive questions, forming the bulk of the qualitative data, were taped and later transcribed for analysis. Follow-up interviews conducted 2 months later were intended to fill gaps not covered in the first round and to explore more carefully issues of management style and attitudes towards success. The short time span between interviews did not allow for diachronic analysis; some significant changes had, however, taken place in many companies even within this short period. The sample was structured to reflect a diversity of industrial and business situations along the following dimensions: industrial sector (traditional, non-traditional and new); life cycle (age and personal situation); business organization; and geographical location (London, Glasgow and Nottingham). Compared with the self-employed population of women as a whole, the sample was skewed towards 'Other Manufacturing' and 'Banking and Financial Services' and away from 'Retail, Distribution, Hotel and Catering' and 'Other Services' sectors. This reflects not only the researchers' concentration on women in non-traditional sectors, but also the patterns of business activity present in the three geographical locations. Companies in the Nottingham area were dominated by those in the 'Other Manufacturing' (clothing) sector, whereas financial services and service-based companies were predominant in London. Construction, chemicals and metals manufacturing were represented in Glasgow. Overall, however, the sample businesses were spread more evenly over a variety of sectors than is the case for the total population of female entrepreneurs and self-employed.

Stratification by age produced a sample more closely related to that of the total population of female business owners. Different age ranges ensured that the sample included women at a variety of stages in their lives. Women who had moved into enterprise from economic activity, older women without children and young women with little experience of employment were deliberately included in the study. The majority of women were married or in stable relationships and just over half had children. The educational backgrounds of the women were, generally, high: 57 women had taken part in full or part-time further education and of these all had obtained at least one qualification. Previous work experience indicates that a majority of respondents were highly motivated towards a career of some kind and most had spent a large proportion of their lives at work. In addition, most had an exceptionally positive attitude towards working (although not necessarily employment). Employment immediately prior to start-up varied considerably: 27 held either managerial or professional posts; five secretarial or clerical and one manual; four came directly from full-time education and 25 were not employed. Eight of the sample were already self-employed prior to starting their current venture. A high proportion of the sample (78%) had some family connection with entrepreneurship during their lifetime.

Firm age was not a determining factor in sample stratification, and the age of the companies varied between less than 1 year and 23 years, the mean age being 2 years. Cross-sectional analysis enabled differentiation by firm age. While a variety of organizational structures was represented, sole traders and partnerships were especially common among the younger businesses; limited companies were favoured by older, more established enterprises. Ten of the partnerships were run in conjunction with other women (usually of a similar age and occupational background). While the final sample did not constitute an exact matrix, the businesses were broadly divided by the various dimensions. The methodology and sample profile are examined in greater depth in the Appendix.

A complete picture of self-employment calls for the issues of failure to be addressed as well as issues of success. In addition to the main sample of 60 business owners, an outriding study was undertaken of 10 women who had been in business, but who had subsequently ceased trading. Reasons for business closure varied between voluntary withdrawal and enforced bankruptcy. As with the main sample, the research techniques used permitted respondents in this category to describe their own experiences and to determine individual definitions of 'success' and 'failure' concepts. Scholars of attribution theories of achievement motivation consistently demonstrate significant gender differences among a variety of occupational groupings (Veroff *et al.*, 1975; Deaux, 1976; Bierhoff-Alfermann, 1977). Although the self-employed have not been subject to this scrutiny, it is likely that differences in the attribution of success and failure noted in other occupational categories are replicated among the self-employed, with women tending to attribute failure to the internal dimensions, defined by Weiner (1972), of 'effort' and 'ability'. The size and scope of this outriding study precluded any substantive conclusions to be drawn. It is, however, interesting to note that the respondents' descriptions generally reinforce the findings of previous studies investigating task success and failure.

It is hypothesized in this study that women can be differentiated by behaviourial and motivational factors in their desire to start in business and, moreover, that these factors influence the process of change. Enterprises owned by the female respondents were frequently established to fulfil personal goals and needs. When these changed the businesses changed accordingly. It was also demonstrated that, among respondents in this study, individual measures of performance were based largely on how well the business met the personal goals of the entrepreneur as opposed to the more conventional commercial criteria of success, such as economic growth, financial stability and job creation.

The results of this study demonstrate that female business proprietors face certain distinctive challenges. The extent to which these are either caused or exacerbated by gender is difficult to quantify. While many self-employed women perceive gender-related problems, others have either different experiences or do not recognize problems as having a gender dimension. Whether these problems are real or based on misconceptions is of little consequence; the perception of a problem, in many cases, is as valid as a 'real' problem. There was a distinct belief among the main sample that barriers were both environmental and inherent within themselves.

Those women who had ceased trading provided interesting comparisons with the main sample regarding entrepreneurial and managerial behaviour and strategies. Especially noticeable, by both its presence in the main sample and its absence in the subsample, was the difference in previous experience of business, management and recent employment. None of the women in the subsample sought to redress this gap in their experience. Only two women sought training in business ownership and management. This is in marked contrast with the main sample. Even those successful women entrepreneurs with management experience still undertook training to compensate for possible deficiencies. Determination to utilize social and business networks efficiently as both a market entry tactic and an ongoing management policy was also a feature of the main sample. These were not features of the behaviour of the unsuccessful proprietors. The subsample were generally ambivalent about the concept of business ownership, although whether this was present prior to embarking in the venture or came about post-failure is unclear. A clear conclusion of the study is that there are certain 'success' strategies which women adopt to counter either direct or indirect barriers to start-up or success. These vary from firm to firm and often depend upon the age and experience of the proprietor. The frequency with which they occur, allied to the systematic way in which they are used, indicates that they have a strong influence on the success of the venture.

2

Starting in Business

This chapter explores why women from a variety of backgrounds move into self-employment and business ownership. Career histories and motivations for business ownership are examined. The diversity which emerges reaffirms the view that there is no 'single entrepreneurial experience' (Goffee and Scase, 1985). Common motivations and barriers do occur, however. These are associated with the previous career experience and the personal or managerial approach of the women starting businesses.

The way women approach starting an enterprise is dominated by the stage they have reached in their life cycle, that is, their age and their domestic relationships. Differentiation by personal life cycle is important as respondents start businesses at very different points in their lives and this affects the types of businesses and their individual approach to business ownership. In addition, the previous domestic and career experience of the respondents was expected to produce different motivations and aspirations for business ownership. Many of the tables in this chapter show a breakdown of respondents by the age of their companies: less than 1 year; 1–5 years; and over 5 years. Analysis by age of company is valuable for two reasons. First, the environment for small business start-up has undergone a dramatic change over the past few years. Increasingly, individuals are publicly urged to take a more entrepreneurial approach to their working lives and there have been significant government and local initiatives to improve the climate for small business start-up. Financial assistance measures, ranging from the Enterprise Allowance Scheme to the Loan Guarantee Scheme, have proliferated. Other forms of help including increasing availability of especially designed premises for business start-ups and more comprehensive advisory services, mean that the experience of business start-up in the 1990s is significantly different from that of 10 or 20 years ago. Second, distinguishing respondents by firm age provides a means to compensate for the

15

methodological problems which can be caused by poor recall of the events which led up to the formation of the business.

The lives and career histories of the women entrepreneurs vary considerably. Most of those identified in this study had undertaken further education. This contrasts markedly with findings about male entrepreneurs and owner-managers. It clashed with the popular 'self-made man' stereotype of the entrepreneur. Successful women entrepreneurs are better educated than either the failed business owners in the parallel study or the total population of women. Most also have pursued some sort of career path, usually in traditionally female employment sectors, such as retailing and service industries. A minority had pursued careers in non-traditional sectors before starting in business. Successful female entrepreneurs were more likely to start businesses in an industry in which they had direct experience than unsuccessful women business owners. They were, however, less likely to start firms in sectors they had worked in before than male business owners. Where they had no direct experience, a deliberate policy to fill gaps in knowledge through training and networking was invariably linked with success. Older respondents tended to believe that it was now easier for women to pursue all types of career paths. This was seen as true even in traditionally male areas such as engineering and construction. One respondent, the owner of a light engineering company, had always wanted to work as an engineer. She had left school at 16 to work in an office, as she said:

> ... it was inconceivable at that time for a girl to work in engineering, although all the boys left school and went straight into apprenticeships at NEL. It was expected of them.

Having worked in an office for 1 year, she too applied and was accepted for an apprenticeship at the National Engineering Laboratories. She then pursued a 15-year career in different light engineering firms. Ultimately she achieved her goal of business ownership by organizing a management buy-out. The route she adopted is the classic entrepreneurial approach adopted in sectors such as engineering. Traditional barriers to entry have made it hard for women to take the first steps to gain knowledge and managerial experience of markets, resources and processes.

Women can break out into non-traditional sectors after a career in traditionally female employment. These women had started businesses within the clothes and textile manufacturing sector in the East Midlands after several years work experience in the industry. Their histories were very similar. Having left school young, their first jobs were as trainee machinists in small local clothes manufacturing firms. After training as machinists, they moved on to work as cutters and designers before eventually becoming involved in supervisory and management positions. This often included managing production and meeting buyers. Most had worked their way up to senior positions in their previous firms before starting on their own. These cases illustrate important and general features of business ownership. They demonstrate the incubator effect of small firms (Fothergill and Gudgin, 1982). Small firms provide the most fertile environment for future generations of new businesses. Experience of an entrepreneurial concern demonstrates that enterprise is attainable. Simultaneously, specialist skills can be developed and opportunities for personal achievement proliferate. These women had pursued careers in traditional female occupations, such as machining, and used that experience to start firms in non-traditional areas of business ownership, such as manufacturing.

Table 2.1 indicates that almost half those running their own business were involved in some form of managerial, professional or entrepreneurial activity while planning their business. These business owners illustrate the strong association between previous experience and the business sector chosen for proprietorship. For most women, career experience was the dominant factor in business ownership; this was especially noticeable among those with managerial experience or indirect experience of business ownership. For other women, the move into self-employment (and the optimum strategy for those without experience of business ownership) was achieved by building the business from hobbies or unpaid domestic skills. Table 2.2 shows the linkages between skills gained in previous employment and their relevance to business ownership. A successful self-employed hairdresser followed a well-trodden path when she left school to train as a hairdresser. Although she had originally started hairdressing as a means of supplementing her pocket

Table 2.1 Occupation while planning the business.

Occupation	No.	%
Senior management	6	11
Junior management	2	4
Technical/professional	12	21
Sales	4	7
Secretarial/clerical	5	8
Manual	1	2
Self-employed	8	13
Unemployed	14	23
Housewife	4	7

Table 2.2 Links between duties/activities, responsibilities and knowledge in new company and last job. Respondents' subjective opinion.

How related	Business age		
	<1 year No.	1–5 years No.	>5 years No.
Unrelated	4	5	1
Moderate relationship	5	9	3
Completely related	8	12	7
Total	17	26	11

Scale 1–7 recoded: 1,2 = unrelated; 3,4,5 = moderately related; 6,7 = substantially/completely related.

money while at school, she was able to earn a more than adequate salary on a full-time basis. Similar histories were told by women operating businesses utilizing self-taught skills. This phenomenon can be seen among male entrepreneurs. It is both more common and more important for women starters. This reflects the more restricted range of career opportunities and the easier move from hobby to low-cost business venture. It poses problems to the developing business. Many hobby-based ventures are attractive because the skills needed and the resources required are generally available and easily accessible. This reduces the scope for competitive advantage, keeps profits low and restricts the scope for growth.

For many women, their current venture is their first experience of business ownership. Those women whose businesses had survived for more than 5 years were different. As Table 2.3 shows, the majority had

Table 2.3 How many times have you owned your own business before now?

	Business age		
	<1 year No.	1–5 years No.	>5 years No.
First time	11	23	6
Once before	5	7	3
Twice or more	2	0	3
Total	18	30	12

Table 2.4 Which came first, the desire to be self-employed or the idea for the business?

	Business age		
	<1 year No.	1–5 years No.	>5 years No.
Self-employment	7	14	3
Business idea	8	8	4
Both at same time	3	8	5
Total	18	30	12

previous experience of business ownership. Experience of ownership can come from other sources. Over three-quarters of the successful women owners (78%) had some family connection with self-employment during their lifetime. Over half had husbands or domestic partners who were self-employed and others came from families where either their mother or father was self-employed. Those with a small business connection were far more likely to be very successful or moderately successful than those lacking prior experience.

As Table 2.4 demonstrates, for some women, the desire for self-employment arose before a specific business idea. Others had a business idea and then started their business. For some women, there was a clear intention and desire to become self-employed. The business idea was generated only after a period of searching for an appropriate mechanism to achieve their ambition. Other women had a good idea and this led them into business ownership. The specific impetus to start in business was often a combination of circumstances occurring at a particular time. This was often a combination of internal and external factors.

The owner of a flexographic printing company described her situation at start up:

> It was being in the right place at the right time. You know I was working in the company and the owner wanted to sell and I knew that I could run it more profitably than it had been in the past and get more satisfaction out of it. So we took the plunge and purchased it when it came on the market. My husband kept his occupation and we took this on as a separate entity so to speak.

For the owner of a clothes manufacturing business, the boredom of her previous job was coupled with a strong desire to have her own business as an outlet for creative energy and talent. With two children of secondary school age and a husband whose salary could support all of them, if necessary, she spent the last 6 months of paid employment planning to start up on her own: writing a business plan; telling buyers that she was starting up by herself; getting advance orders; finding premises; raising capital from her bank; and latterly advertising for staff.

> To be free, to take the risk is almost like painting a picture. It's creating something which I think has got some art in it. It is setting things in place and seeing them grow. You are able to put your ideas into practice, they don't all work, rather than that, it's a creative activity.

Many women stated that, although they had harboured a desire for self-employment for a long period, the specific stimulus to start up was a single event. Most cited events such as redundancy or a specific career frustration as the impetus.

Others, however, cited a change in their personal circumstances, such as marriage, divorce or pregnancy as the event which led them to re-evaluate their working lives. For many, the events which led up to self-employment were traumatic. Almost one in three respondents indicated that business start-up was a response to being a "victim of some traumatic event". Similar processes have been identified, but far less often, among male entrepreneurs.

Being passed over for promotion in her job as a full-time union official led one woman to start a management consultancy business specializing in the implementation of equal opportunities policies.

> I had worked with them for ten years—I was the Union's Scottish coordinator—I knew more about implementing equal opportunities than any one of them—and they advertised this post. It was blatantly obvious that it was for me, and they gave it to some man who knew nothing at all about the job. Yes, it was traumatic and yes I damn well did feel victimized.

Dismissal spurred another:

> There had been some trouble in the company for a few months, you know, things being ripped off and they didn't know who it was although it had to be someone pretty high up. Ken (co-director) and I worked it out though, who it could be. So we went to the Chairman and told him of our suspicions and he said that he knew that it was the Managing Director, he knew who it was, but that he needed him in the company, he couldn't let him go. Then, a week later, he came to us and said that he didn't think that we could go on working in the company knowing what we did about the MD and that he would have to let us go . . . after we had been unemployed for five months a friend of ours wanted to sell his business and came and asked us if we were interested. We were really surprised, really shocked, we had never thought that we could start up by ourselves. We looked into it, you know, but really it was much too expensive . . . it was only then that we realized that we could start up by ourselves.

For many, business ownership was the result of reassessing their lives after a specific event: redundancy, threat of redundancy, divorce, or a particular event at work which led to unfair dismissal. Few, however, felt that proprietorship was a negative reaction; rather it was seen to be a positive step after a possibly negative experience.

Motivations for Business Ownership

Over the past decade a number of studies have examined the motivations for self-employment (Scott, 1980; Scase and Goffee, 1980, 1982; Gibb and Ritchie, 1982). This body of research invariably focuses upon the search for independence, or as Scott (1980) expresses it: "the flight from the large scale as a means of personal fulfilment". With few exceptions these studies used male respondents. The underlying assumption is either that women did not pursue this type of career and were, therefore, not worthy of investigation or that if they did, their motivations for starting in business would replicate the findings of male entrepreneurs. Current evidence suggests that female motivations for business ownership may be different from their male counterparts.

The most common reasons given for entering into business, super-ficially at least, mirror the findings of studies using male respondents (Table 2.5). 'Independence' and 'the challenge of business ownership' are

Table 2.5 Reasons for self-employment (summary of most important reasons).

	Business age		
Most important reason	<1 year No.	1–5 years No.	>5 years No.
Desire for*			
Independence	12	20	7
The challenge	4	4	2
Unemployment	0	2	1
Others	2	4	2
To earn lots more money	0	0	0
Total	18	30	12

* "To be own boss/not told what to do/profits not going to someone else/ rewards for self/choose when to work/choose who to work for/escape from large firm".

the two most cited reasons. A single notion of independence, however, masks the complexities of the issue. Women at different stages of their lives cited the need for independence from a variety of different circumstances. Five distinct groups of respondents could be broadly identified from an analysis of the data explaining issues of motivation. Their experiences are described below.

For some young women, independence meant freedom from the confines of the formal labour market. Self-employment offers greater career opportunities for this group than employment and is seen as a long term career option. Typically, they moved straight into proprietorship from advanced full-time education with vacation work providing their only previous employment experience. Through self-employment, they were able to create their own career paths and fulfil their ambitions. Some of these women described their experience:

> This is the best time to do it, once you've left college because you have so little to survive on at the beginning, you are used to living on so little money.

> I had always thought, even back at school, that I would one day have my own business. Basically, it's independence, I just wanted to do what I wanted to do. Not wanting to be told what to do any more.

Some proprietors of art and craft-based businesses stated that they had been encouraged to move into self-employment during their degree courses. One ceramic designer said:

> I was at the college and the sort of degree I did encouraged you to have your own workshop when you left and carry on working on your own. It [self-employment] was already inbred in the sort of Art School mentality.

These businesses ranged from manufacturing through to craft and design businesses and service companies. Their ambitions for business success did not lead them to identify profits as a reason for self-employment. Success was seen in terms of personal integrity and survival. Profits and growth were, initially at least, seen as an external confirmation of their ability, rather than a primary goal. One fabric designer pointed out:

> I like to maintain and meet my demands on time. That is the only thing I worry about all the time. I believe in having a good business name, my integrity and the work and the product have to be of the highest quality at all times. If something is not at that level I do not sell it.

Young entrepreneurs tend to be more common during periods of rapid economic change. The emergence of these younger, first generation, business starters is a relatively new phenomenon. Not all the women in the younger age groups are equally determined to achieve business ownership or ambitious for business success. Some are self-employed or sole proprietors of businesses in traditionally female sectors such as catering, where ease of market entry is a determining factor of business choice. Many had drifted into self-employment for a series of reasons. Often they reject the conventional employer/employee relationship typified by the formal labour market. Paradoxically this can stem from a fear of failure and a belief that they lack the motivation and ambition necessary to compete in larger firms. Attitudes to self-employment, or any form of capital accumulation, are also equivocal. Often financed solely by parents, self-employment is seen as a temporary means of earning a modest living after finishing full-time education. For this group of respondents the term 'independence' is a rejection of traditional authority figures without a positive acceptance of self-determination.

One self-employed woman whose business is based on designing and printing logos for sweatshirts said:

> I didn't think about self-employment until six months ago . . . at college I couldn't bear the idea of having to work for anybody else, so after I graduated I came back here to live with my parents and was unemployed for nine months. It was then that my parents started talking about me starting a business and they just went out and bought these machines for me and booked me on a training course one weekend. It was they that got me this workspace and everything.

> I have never been for a job interview, never filled in an application form. Just doing a proper job was something that never, ever occurred to me. Really, both of us happened to be in the right place at the right time. Neither of us had anything particularly special to do. I have never considered the option of buying a newspaper and applying for every job, I'm sure I would hate work like that.

This group of women are 'pushed' into self-employment. All were unemployed before starting up. Unemployment, however, is not the sole determining factor in the self-employment decision. More positive, 'pull' factors such as a desire for autonomy are also cited by these respondents as motivations. Positive experiences during start-up can strengthen their determination to succeed and overcome early ambivalence about self-employment. Negative experiences after market entry could, of course, produce the opposite effect.

> Control over my own environment is very important. I didn't particularly want to start a business and it wasn't that I wanted independence and control, I found myself sort of thrust into this. But, now that I am in it, I find

those things very valuable and that is why I would hate to give it up now, the independence and control of my life.

The older age groups in the sample included women who started in business after a successful career. These were usually in a managerial or professional capacity. For them, the independence of proprietorship was desired for several reasons. Many of these achievement-orientated women had suffered the frustration of gender-related career blocks, the so-called 'glass ceiling' effect (Hymounts, 1986), demonstrated by a lack of recognition and progression within the company, beyond a certain level.

One architect describes it thus:

> The problems I didn't expect to find were my employers not seeing me as management potential. I found it very difficult to ask for pay rises, more seniority, though I find it easy to take on responsibility in the office. I ended up running the biggest job and having a very senior position as regards responsibility, but not given that as regards money or status. That was one of the reasons why I decided to set up on my own.

Similar circumstances are described by other women:

> I got, like a lot of women, so fed up with working for other people. You are doing all this work for them preparing your boss for meetings, and he comes out shining and he's probably contributed very little.

> I'm not good at working for anyone else as I tend to do things my way. That doesn't always do in a large organization.

> Going into self-employment did give me the opportunity to reach my potential and I don't think I would have got that in a conventional company, small or large.

> I had been through the hoop before, of kicking myself out of the secretarial rut and getting out of it and thought I don't really want to get back into it. I can't have children, my husband is away a great deal. So I thought the answer is self-employment.

Many of these women were disillusioned with traditional employer/employee relationships. They felt their chosen careers had failed them despite their apparent success. Other women in this group wanted the flexibility to have both a family and a career. This was not available to them as employees. Starting businesses allowed them the opportunity to have children without incurring penalties in their careers. They had been failed by the formal labour market and sought to redress this through proprietorship.

One woman described the reaction of her former employers on learning of her pregnancy:

... he was quite horrified and I was told that if it stood in any way, shape or form between my job I would have to go. Two days after my son was born, I had a phone call at six thirty at night to say that I was working the next day.

Other successful career-orientated women simply found conventional employment frustrating and sought independence and autonomy. Their businesses tended to be in non-traditional sectors such as manufacturing and engineering. Like other respondents in this group, their aspirations for the business were high. Business ownership for them is, in practice, a career substitute.

I had worked in this company for twenty years, I had started out as a machinist and worked my way up to director in charge of design. But the owner had reached a stage where he just wanted the company to tick along and stay just as it was and you just can't do that in the rag trade. I was so bored and I had so many ideas which he rejected totally out of hand. It was clear for me that if I wanted to get on with them I would have to start my own company. Now I'm his biggest competitor—that's made him move!

The company is not that important. It's the vehicle I'm travelling in at the moment. It could be anything, it could be on my own. It's the freedom to do the job I am doing, without restrictions, or without my not being heard or dismissed as not important.

The growing importance of management buy-outs as a route to self-employment can be seen among female entrepreneurs. Several women organized management buy-outs after closures were threatened. They emphasized that it was not just independence and profitability that prompted this but possible job losses for others and the risk of letting clients and customers down.

The owner of a merchandising firm described her previous employers and the takeover situation:

Nobody had got any idea how to run a merchandising team. I was brought in with my knowledge to set it all up and they had got no idea. They were all very much anti-women, their attitude was "why is a woman doing this job, it should be a man". I had a lot of obstacles to get over, they were male chauvinistic pigs at all levels, from management down to shop floor. Although they knew that they had to employ part-time women, they called them housewives. They would turn round and say "who would employ housewives", they were very, very nasty. They thought a woman should be at home with an apron and tied to the kitchen sink. That was their kind of attitude ...

They did a massive reorganization within the company and decided that the merchandising service along with a lot of the reps had to go. I was horrified, to me it was very profitable, I think that there were a lot of politics involved. I have always wanted to have, aimed at having my own business. But at the end of the day when there was this situation of the public or the clients losing, not being able to have their work covered and also forty girls going to be made redundant, I thought well, now is the time.

A Glasgow-based engineer had a similar experience:

> There was this big union dispute and they decided that the plant would have to go. Three of us got together for the buy-out—me and two men. . . . One of the men was a real pain, and really just started to expect more money from the business which it couldn't really afford at the time, so the other two of us bought his share of the company. It really wasn't working out for him. Then the other man, my second partner, had a heart attack ten months later—couldn't take the strain—so I bought him out to become sole owner. At that point the company was losing money. One year later I had paid off all our debts, which came to about £50 000 and made a modest profit to boot. We've been expanding consistently since then.

The proprietor of a small antiques restoration workshop converted an unprofitable limited company into a profitable workers co-operative.

> We were made redundant so we had to do something. It just seemed silly to turn down the opportunity of a workshop with customers on your books and things, with a four month waiting list of work coming in. It just seemed stupid to turn it down, it was just a question of how to do it, get the money to keep it going.

These self-descriptions and the entrepreneurial response are consistent with Schien's (1978) view that prior dissatisfaction with career opportunities or lifestyle is a major precondition for entrepreneurial activity. It suggests that the trigger of dissatisfaction is more important for women entrepreneurs in the UK than has emerged in non-gender research. Gibb and Ritchie (1982) argue in the wider context that: "There was indeed little support for the notion that it was dissatisfaction with present career opportunity that led to entrepreneurial activity". Clearly, in the cases reported here, these frustrations provided at least the immediate stimulus to action.

Returners

Female returners are an increasingly important entrepreneurial group. Self-employment is an accessible means of returning to economic activity after a period devoted to motherhood. Few of the returners interviewed can be been classified as 'domestics', as defined by Goffee and Scase (1985), running small-scale businesses in traditional sectors. Not only were they strongly committed to entrepreneurship, but they were often the most radical in their feminist beliefs. While businesses in the short term were designed to suit domestic responsibilities, most were ambitious for the businesses to grow.

Returners or 're-entrants' often came out of established career paths to have children. Typically, they had started businesses on a part-time basis, sometimes in partnership with women in similar circumstances. Businesses are started with the intention of becoming long-term careers, after the perception that they cannot return easily to mainstream employment. This group of respondents is often the most committed and motivated towards business ownership. Their businesses had to be kept deliberately small for a long period of time before the women running them were able and confident to make them a full-time occupation. For them, proprietorship offers short-term independence from motherhood as well as a long-term career strategy.

> I enjoy it, I enjoy it immensely and the reason for having my own business was that it was something I could get involved in and would enjoy. I don't see the company as a great big enterprise.

> I think that it is quite nice to have the control and to people your office with whom you want to work with and to create your own working environment. . . . I think ownership probably gives you quite a lot of status, which is something that I probably quite like and the confidence you gain from that.

For those women who came from families where self-employment was prevalent, proprietorship was both a positive and a traditional way of life. They are usually older (over 45) and share many experiences with both returners and the high achievement groups. Typically, they have direct personal experience of small business management through a family business. Their perceptions of self-employment are quite different from those held by other female business proprietors. Business ownership, for this group of women, is seen as the norm, employment the exception. Independence as a motivating factor implies a return to or adoption of a 'normal' way of life. For some women, their only experience of employment had been within family-owned firms.

> My father's self-employed, well, he has a freight haulage firm and I worked for him for a few years and then after I had learnt more about TM [transcendental meditation] and yoga I started teaching that full-time, well,

on a freelance basis. I met my husband that way, he's self-employed too. Then I started this company and that has been going for a couple of years.

I always thought that I could do well on my own and my family have always had businesses. Even though my father is now employed, he runs a school. His mother started a school. My mother's family are all butchers, so the self-employment thing has always been around.

Motivations for starting in business, although nominally described as 'a search for independence' vary. They usually depend on the background and previous experience of the individual. The respondents can be divided into five groups by their common experiences and motivations for start-up. These are: *aspirants*, young achievement-orientated women who view proprietorship as a long-term career option; *accidentalists*, young women who drift into self-employment; *high achievers*, older, achievement-orientated women who move into business ownership to satisfy career ambitions—which often enables domestic circumstances to change; *re-entrants*, women returning to economic activity; and *traditionalists*, women for whom self-employment is an established way of life. This classification of respondents does not constitute a typology but was used as an analytical tool to identify similarities and patterns of behaviour. In this sense, the use resembles Weberian 'ideal types'. They are, however, behaviourial classifications which focus upon motivations at the pre-start and start-up stages of entrepreneurship and not categories which respondents necessarily belong to for any extended period. The dynamic nature of female entrepreneurship requires a system of classification which can absorb change and vary with adaptations to the behaviour and views of respondents. Respondents can change to different modes of entrepreneurial behaviour when circumstances change or conditions require novel responses. This 'style flexibility' is a crucial feature of the success strategy of effective entrepreneurship.

The groupings are not performance related *per se* and are not indicators of the level of eventual success. Inevitably, the respondents' experiences of business start-up, the barriers they face and the ways these are overcome are inextricably linked to their background and motivations.

CASE STUDY

Company activity: *Wire Design and Manufacture*
Company started: *1981*
Employees: *22*
Business organization: *Limited Company*

Company History

An industrial dispute at her former employers which led to the threatened closure of the plant, a branch of a multinational engineering company, forced this respondent to consider a management buy-out with two male colleagues. The three partners put equal financing of £10 000 into the venture which bought machinery and the existing order book, besides other company assets, although not the company name. Within a year the respondent had bought out one partner. Two years after the new business started, the respondent bought out the second partner to wholly own the business. At this point the company was technically insolvent, having made a large loss in the second year of operation. The respondent diversified the product range, moving away from mass markets where she could not compete with imported goods and into specialist niches. Within 10 months of total buy-out, the respondent had cleared outstanding debts and made a modest end-of-year profit. Since then the company, producing wire for specialist markets, has increased turnover and profitability every year of operation.

Starting Up

The respondent had a long held ambition for self-employment prior to starting her current business, and although she had plenty of ideas for self-employment, considered them too weak. The industrial dispute at her former employers provided her with a suitable entry into profitable business ownership.

Having decided to go ahead with the buy-out, the respondent approached her bank manager for £2000 top-up funding to supplement her personal savings of £8000. He refused additional finance on the basis that he did not lend to women who wished to start in business. He did, however, add that he would have lent her the money if she wished to buy a car. She then approached a different bank, whose manager had lent the full equity needed for her two partners. He agreed to lend her the additional finance, providing that her husband guaranteed the loan. She accepted the offer although resented the need for a guarantee given the amount she, personally, was investing. Since that point she has stayed with that bank, although every loan has required security. Her husband, who subsequently joined the company as a non-executive director, is no longer required to guarantee loans.

Within a year of sole ownership, the company had expanded to a point where it could no longer trade satisfactorily from the original premises, an industrial site of 1200 square feet. Larger premises (3800 square feet) were sought near the original site to allow for further growth and expansion.

The company started on a full-time basis both to revitalize the plant and to service existing customers brought from the original owners. For this respondent, starting in business would have been easier in retrospect had she achieved the buy-out single handedly. She feels that the presence of her two former partners hampered start-up and growth to the extent that the company was unable to trade sufficiently for the first few years.

This respondent stated that she approached several advisory agencies when completing the buy-out and has since made use of local authority and Development Agency personnel for specific problems, such as premises and employment grants. While ongoing help has been useful for the company, especially from sector-specific advisors, start-up assistance from the Small Firms Service was disappointing. She perceived the service to be more suitable for smaller firms with lower aspirations, but in her experience they "gave you an umbrella when the sun is shining".

Growth and Development

The respondent has planned carefully for growth and states that she has clear objectives for the company for the next 10 years which include continual growth and expansion. For her, the continual development of the company is a clear priority and the possible contraction of the company to accommodate personal circumstances is anathema to her. Currently, her main objective is to ensure a successful move into new purpose-built premises of 11 500 square feet to allow for further growth and development.

Unable to compete with imported goods in the mass market, she has carefully developed quality products in more specialized market niches. She feels strongly that manufacturing businesses are not encouraged nor given specific incentives and tax breaks to compete effectively. When asked what government support would be useful to help her establish her business, her response was a lowering of interest rates for manufacturing firms coupled with a surcharge upon imported goods.

Barriers and Strategies for Success

This respondent experienced several barriers when starting her business, most of which she was able to overcome effectively. Strategies for success initially included using male business partners to front the company, "a strategy successful in the beginning for start-up, which soon became a liability when I had to work with them", followed by one of professionalization. She now feels that she has become so established and successful that she can accommodate any current and future problems. Certainly her success has given her a great deal of confidence in herself, her business skills and the future of her company. She now feels that her gender gives her power of surprise when meeting people external to the business, although she stresses that she has always been a fighter, prepared to tackle anything. Her twin motivations when starting the business were to "earn lots more money" and the "challenge of business ownership". The challenging aspect of ownership was cited as the main reason.

Specific problems included childcare provision for her 8-year-old daughters. This she has resolved by asking her mother to look after the children out of school hours. The guilt of not being with them completely is, however, partially offset by the extra income achieved and the benefit of being a role model to her daughters.

Ongoing problems cited by this respondent include staff recruitment and employee relations. Anti-trade unions, she believes that management and staff have common aims and objectives and that there can be no place for trade unions or staff associations within small companies. The majority of her employees are female and she adopts a deliberate policy of employing women for two reasons. First, she believes they work harder than men and are easier to manage. Second, she wants to encourage women into non-traditionally female areas such as engineering. This respondent has experienced managerial problems with male employees; one of her most senior employees is reluctant to take orders from her, a reaction, she perceives, related to her gender. She resolves this problem by channelling requests through her husband, a procedure she finds irritating but amusing, rather than threatening.

3

Planning the Business

Once the decision to start a business is made, new challenges and demands emerge. Respondents faced a number of choices regarding preparation and planning for business ownership. In this chapter, the different approaches taken by women business owners are investigated. Their ability to mobilize resources for start-up is a crucial determinant of long-term viability and success. All respondents recognized that the start-up period is crucial to the long-term success of the business. Many took great care in planning for start-up and preparing a business plan. The amount of time allowed for this varied considerably (Table 3.1). The majority took up to 6 months planning the business, although some took more than 2 years. In the case of three management buy-outs, respondents took only 1 month between announcements of company closure and the successful take-over of the company. The time taken was not a major determinant of eventual success. Shorter, more intensive periods of preparation linked with a background knowledge of an industry can be

Table 3.1 How long did you seriously consider self-employment before your business finally started?

| | Business age | | |
	<1 year No.	1–5 years No.	>5 years No.
Less than 1 month	0	3	1
1–6 months	12	22	7
6–12 months	4	2	2
1–2 years	2	2	1
2–5 years	0	1	1
Total	18	30	12

Table 3.2 Spare time planning and part-time trading.

	Business age		
	<1 year No.	1–5 years No.	>5 years No.
Yes, planned business in spare time	13	15	9
No, did not	5	15	3
Total	18	30	12
Started trading Part-time	9	9	3
Full-time	9	21	9
Total	18	30	12

as valuable as a long period of gestation. The processes undertaken, planning, research and relevant training are more important than the length of time.

A large majority of the successful women entrepreneurs had planned their new businesses in their spare time while continuing in previous jobs. As Table 3.2 shows, a significant minority had traded on a part-time basis before starting full time. They saw many benefits of part-time trading. Several viewed part-time trading as an experimental and developmental approach to business. It is akin to the 'test market' period for a new product or service. The key components of the new venture, the product, the target market, the costs and prices could be varied to get an ideal mix. Failure could be contained within acceptable bounds and the true nature of the opportunity could be understood. This 'test market' was especially successful when a flexible or adaptive response was taken to market information and perceived weaknesses in the business. It cured perspective proprietors of the often fatal 'it will be alright on the night' syndrome.

For others, notably the returners, part-time trading was not a test or experiment, it was a distinct phase in the emergence of the enterprise until domestic circumstances allowed full-time ownership. For some, however, it is neither financially possible nor desirable to maintain this transitional status for long. Having planned their businesses over several months, most achievement-orientated women started trading on a full-time basis as early as possible, one stating that "if you are serious, it is the only way to do it". A clothes manufacturer from Nottingham commented:

I would say thinking big and financing accordingly is the best approach to start-up. I mean, if you are serious then you have to commit yourself 100%. But really our approach was starting small and expanding very rapidly without over-trading.

This ambitious growth orientation was an intrinsic feature of the goal set of the larger ventures. Continued development, the search for new opportunities and personal dedication is a powerful combination.

Prior experience of failure has been identified in earlier non-gender-based research as an important learning experience. This research has tended to concentrate on the positive, learning and awareness gains from this experience of failure. This was confirmed, but a rather harsher dimension to the experience of failure emerged.

A London-based industrial photographer was compelled to start in business on a full-time basis to service debts from her previous business which had failed. She described her attitudes to starting in business again and also the benefit of her previous experience:

It's been a bit daunting starting up on my own, because I have this amazing debt hanging over me. But, luckily, I have now got the experience of knowledge—I know now to bring in the teams according to the job. I know now how to do it and where to go.

US experience of the reconstructed business would suggest that this approach is far more common in North America than in Britain.

The Business Plan

Most women prepare an initial business plan (Table 3.3). Interestingly, more of the newer businesses had prepared formal plans for business start-up than women with more established businesses. Over 90% of the newer businesses had prepared a business plan. This compares with 73%

Table 3.3 Did you prepare a business plan?

	Business age		
	<1 year No.	1–5 years No.	>5 years No.
Yes	17	22	13
No	1	8	7
Total	18	30	20

and 67% respectively of the businesses aged between 1 and 5 years and older. This concentration upon business planning probably reflects the business training which most had sought. The increased general awareness of the value of planning seems to be having an effect on business behaviour. The newer businesses used the plan to guide their future behaviour beside reviewing the strengths and weaknesses. Those entering relatively new territory used the material gathered for the plan to compensate for the gaps in their technical or market knowledge. The extent of prior preparation by women business owners is far greater than seems to occur among male business starters. In part, this reflects their relative lack of knowledge of the market or product. Male entrepreneurs are more likely to be entering business areas in which they have direct commercial experience. Using Ansoff's strategic planning grid (Fig. 3.1), they are more likely to be facing the problems of 'diversification' than 'penetration'. This implies that they will require more formal market knowledge and have less opportunity for competitive advantage. There seems to be a powerful, explicit gender dimension to this highly formalized planning. In part this reflects a desire to reassure bankers and other professionals by preparing detailed plans.

Many women felt that advisers such as bankers and accountants are less willing to take business knowledge for granted and give them the benefit of the doubt. The owner of a language and marketing training consultancy planned extensively at start-up. Her response typified the initial benefits of this:

> In the start-up period I would say quite honestly that I handled things very well indeed. I knew where I was going, I knew what I had to do, the training

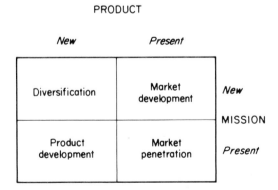

Figure 3.1   Ansoff's strategic planning grid (from Ansoff, 1987, p. 109).

courses that I ran were very well received and there was a tremendous amount of nervousness about whether my ideas were acceptable ... I did sensible things like I sorted out an accountant, I went and saw the bank manager. So there was no point within the first 6 months that I thought that I was doing anything disastrously wrong.

A stained glass designer and manufacturer emphasized the value of a business plan:

You can sit and put down everything. In actual fact it's realistic in that it is for our information, it's not just for the bank. But the point is that it also gives you an idea as to what you have to achieve, and it gives you something to measure the business against. You know if it's not working well. If you have outlined the different areas that you want to move into then you are in a much stronger position to move quickly, if the opportunity presents itself.

Those who had invested time and energy into their plan became strong advocates of their value.

Fears and Concerns

Even with extensive planning, women running businesses express a variety of different concerns about starting in business and its impact on their lives. These ranged from practical concerns about their ability to master basic business skills, such as book-keeping, to the more difficult to resolve and long-term issues such as the availability of capital and the effect of self-employment upon their families (Table 3.4).

Even the achievement-orientated women with previous management experience found starting in business a daunting prospect. A Glasgow-based management consultant commented:

I think that feeling that you are wholly responsible is a very important step, even if the size of the operation you are running isn't any bigger, the fact that you have total responsibility is important. So, although I had some experience beforehand it felt like starting from scratch. You are having to think about contracts and employment and job descriptions and how much you are going to pay people, cash flows of the business, which weren't things that I had really had experience of at this level before.

The search for independence is inextricably linked with a sense of responsibility. Earlier, non-gender-based studies have highlighted the 'loneliness of the long distance entrepreneur'. The spouse and other family support has been presented as an important source of reassurance. Women seem less able to rely on this. At the same time, social reassurance

Table 3.4 Which of the following were you most concerned about before starting business?*

	Business age		
Concerns	<1 year No.	1–5 years No.	>5 years No.
How to do it	4	7	0
Where to get advice	5	5	1
Obtaining capital	10	16	2
Finding property	2	6	3
Getting business	8	16	6
Competition	4	9	3
Pricing product	12	20	7
No guaranteed income	7	11	5
Losing savings	5	3	3
Cash flow	10	10	3
Managing a business	4	5	3
Marketing problems	8	6	2
Taxation problems	7	13	3
VAT problems	6	10	2
Book-keeping	10	8	2
National Insurance	5	6	0
Pension/sickness	3	5	2
Employing people	6	7	3
Effect on family	7	10	3

* Multiple responses.

is harder to find as the wider community finds it harder to acknowledge and legitimize proprietorship as a female pursuit.

Training

Many respondents sought to overcome initial fears about self-employment by attendance at specialist small business management training courses (Table 3.5). These were usually offered by local colleges or by local enterprise agencies. There was a high attendance rate among respondents. It is hard to determine the extent to which this result may be attributable to sampling techniques used. The sources of respondents in this study might produce this effect, however similar samples of male entrepreneurs recruited on the same basis have not produced these results. Many placed the greatest value on the practical topics

Table 3.5   Experience in the following business skills *before intending* and attendance at training courses *after deciding* to go into business.

Area	Experience before intending				Attending training courses after deciding			
	Yes		No		Yes		No	
	No.	%	No.	%	No.	%	No.	%
Management	29	48	31	52	20	33	40	67
Finance	21	35	39	65	27	45	33	55
Book-keeping	21	35	39	65	26	43	34	57
Sales	27	45	33	55	27	45	33	55
Marketing	23	38	37	62	27	45	33	55
Business planning	14	23	46	77	28	47	32	53
None of above	16	27	44	73	27	45	33	55

covered by these courses, for example dealing with VAT, national insurance, and book-keeping. All found the training to be beneficial. One respondent summed up the feelings of many:

> I found the financial and the tax side frightening, and ended up seeking proper advice and finding someone who could do it for me. I think initially, if I'm honest, I thought that I would be doing it all myself and I think that is one of the things you believe. If you're going to go into business, you believe your ideas are right, I'm a positive person and it wasn't easy. Things like the number of forms you have to fill in, the VAT returns, people worrying you all the time about buying typewriters, basically these are trivial things that mean you're not even trying to sell the business, let alone doing it.

Another woman, the owner of a growing data processing agency, received training in market research which enabled her to pursue a niche marketing approach to this sector.

> Because of the view that it was a declining market, many firms have actually gone out of business, but I saw the need that there was still a market, but it was a changed market, much more professional with a lot more capital investment in training and so on. The whole business had to be professional. It was a different environment and, thankfully, my tactics and marketing have proven to be correct.

The networking opportunities of training were praised and given greater emphasis by respondents than in similar non-gender-based research. In part this reflects their shortage of business contacts and their lack of experience of commercial intermediaries. One respondent intending to start a language and marketing training consultancy found that the enterprise agency which suggested basic training in business skills were also able to find financial backing for her business. Others found that banks and institutional lenders were more willing to offer start-up capital after training had been undertaken.

Mobilizing Resources For Start-Up

The search for the resources to underwrite the business, see it through the early years and finance setbacks is common to all new businesses. The challenges faced by women have much in common with men. Women do, however, face distinctive difficulties and lack access to specific sources. Their initial problems centred around the availability of finance, premises and supporting services. Many cite the difficulties they experienced in mobilizing resources for start-up, as especially acute. These are particularly severe in the raising of capital with little access to security for loans and a reluctance to use the family home as security. Experiences varied and often reflected the different backgrounds, aspirations and start-up strategies of the respondents.

Finance

The amount of start-up capital varied widely (Table 3.6). Some start their business with no more than an overdraft facility complemented by the

Table 3.6   How much capital was the business started with?

	Business age		
	<1 year	1–5 years	>5 years
	No.	No.	No.
Less than £1000	2	4	2
£1000–£1999	4	7	1
£2000–£4999	5	3	1
£5000–£9999	2	4	1
£10 000–£19 999	3	5	3
£20 000–£50 000	1	4	3
More than £50 000	1	3	1
Total	18	30	12

Enterprise Allowance Scheme. Others had invested in excess of £50 000. The older, more established businesses had employed a noticeably higher amount of initial capital investment. Much of the variation is accounted for by sectoral differences. Many of the established businesses are capital intensive manufacturing or engineering firms. The primary use of start-up capital was the acquisition of machinery and equipment and buying or converting premises before trading commenced.

The low cost of entry in some sectors made exit quite easy. Those women with clearly defined and well-planned businesses were able to raise the funds to finance their venture. There is no absolute financial barrier to entry. The majority of those who sought external funding used bank overdrafts or bank loans as their major form of start-up capital. This reflects the pattern which can be discerned for all start-ups (Table 3.7). There was very little use of equity finance. It is notable that women required their husband's guarantee before funding was released by a financial institution. In three cases, respondents were successful in gaining backing from venture capital companies. A further five were backed by regional development agencies. For most respondents personal savings formed the bulk of their starting capital, in some cases supplemented by investment by friends and family. This dependence on personal finance left them undercapitalized and vulnerable to changes in trading conditions.

Table 3.7   How was start-up capital made up?

	Business age		
	<1 year No.	1–5 years No.	>5 years No.
Bank overdraft	5	9	3
Bank loan	3	5	3
Husband's guarantee	2	0	0
Venture capital	1	2	0
Finance company	0	1	1
Family	0	4	4
Friends	1	2	1
Inheritance	1	0	1
Personal savings	10	16	5
Mortgage	0	1	1
Development agency	1	4	0
Shareholders	0	1	0
Combination of above	6	11	5

Knowledge of the range and form of financial support was poor. Many share the popular misconception that grant aid or subsidies were widely available. Some women sought grants from funds administered by local authorities or development agencies. Virtually none were backed by local authorities. Generally this reflected the tendency of women-owned businesses to be concentrated in retailing or the services. The owners of a private language school described the problem:

> When we first made enquiries, we said what is there available and they said "Oh dear, you don't produce anything. There are lots of things, lots of help even for exporting, all sorts of things but you don't produce anything". "Well come on", I said, "we are a service, surely education and tourism are two of the biggest invisible exports that we have". But there was nothing on offer that we could identify for which we would be eligible.

Respondents were poorly informed and inexperienced at seeking and using financial and other intermediaries. Most women business owners face difficulties in raising capital to start in business (Table 3.8). The older, more established businesses reported the greatest problems. It does seem that the search process for this funding is both longer and more intensive for women than for their male counterparts. Providers of external finance were loathe to take track records into account. Despite this several raised significant sums. Two-thirds of women whose businesses were over 5 years old reported problems in raising finance, compared with 63% and 50% of businesses aged between 1–5 years and under 1 year. The relative ease of raising finance for the newer ventures reflects the small amounts of funding sought rather than changes in attitudes towards female proprietorship. Of the businesses under 1 year old, 61% of owners had started with less than £5000, compared with 46% and 33% of businesses aged 1–5 years and above. The owner of a literary agency explained the importance of having sufficient financial backing:

Table 3.8 Did you have any problems in arranging start-up finance?

	Business age		
	<1 year No.	1–5 years No.	>5 years No.
Yes	9	19	8
No	9	11	4
Total	18	30	12

If you are trying to set up on your own, you have got to survive. If I hadn't a little finance behind me, I would not have survived. In the first year I made seventeen hundred pounds, the second year sixteen hundred and the third year two thousand. As your reputation builds you get more clients. But again, as I see it, it took about 5 years to make it into something. They were lean years.

Many felt that their gender made lenders reluctant to provide finance. Bank managers and other lenders gave the impression that they did not see women as credible business proprietors. Women business owners expressed the same sentiment in many ways. One said:

It was a tremendous problem. There were three shareholders each who put in a cash sum. This left a sum of £35 000 to be found. To do this, the company purchased its own shares so therefore we needed bank support to the company to the tune of £35 000 over and above the overdraft facilities and the loans that were already in being. The problems we met were with the bank. Their main bone of contention was not the fact that I couldn't run the company, in their opinion that is, but the fact that I was female and this was quite clearly said to us, that was to my husband and myself when we went along to sort all this out. It was clearly because I was female.

Another commented:

I had all these awful interviews with the bank. Oh! we can't lend you money because you are a woman. Your husband has to sign this and whatnot. I think this undermined my confidence and because we didn't get any business the whole thing became the craziest idea I've ever had. Funnily enough, once I got the first piece of business it all started to fall into place. I think I got my confidence back . . . you suddenly didn't think you were such a wally and that you hadn't got it all wrong.

This theme was further elaborated with the observation:

When the bank manager was talking about taking second charge of the house he kept checking that my husband knew that I was thinking about this. Was my husband agreeable? Which is fair enough because we are joint owners of the house but I felt would they ask a man the same question?

Those who succeeded soon found that careful prior preparation was the key to success. They learnt to anticipate difficulties that would be raised. They responded by preparing well for interviews with potential lenders. This meant thorough research into markets and careful technical appraisal and attention to detail. Some sent business plans in advance of meetings.

An overtly professional approach is a crucial feature of the achievement-orientated women to gain confidence and credibility from the lender for the benefit of the enterprise. They adopted the classic negotiating strategy of separating the people from the problem. In these cases it meant separating their gender from the business proposal. They saw the fact that they were women as a problem to be overcome. As a strategy it was not always successful. An engineer explained her problems when organizing a management buy-out:

> Well, we needed £10 000 each. The two men took the business plan to their bank managers and raised the money no problem. I really didn't think that I would have any problem either, you see I had £8000 of my own personal savings—which were nothing to do with my husband—plus the house is in my name not his. So I went to my bank manager, told him about the buy-out, showed him the business plan and asked him for the extra £2000 that I needed, and he said no, he just turned me down flat. I was absolutely furious, I just couldn't believe it. So I said to him, if I had wanted the money for a car loan would he give it to me and he said, well, of course I would, it's just that we don't lend to women for business ventures. I then went to the next bank, the same branch where one of the men got his loan and I got the money from him. But, having said that, although he gave me the money he had belt and braces attached. He even insisted that I would need my husband to act as a guarantor . . . even after I said that the house was in my name. Crazy.

The response of this entrepreneur reflects that of many others. She persisted despite the obstacle. She was willing to accept the negative reaction and continued her search for funds until she got the backing required. This persistence in the face of adversity is a recurring theme in the literature on business ownership.

Not all women shared these experiences of raising capital. A partner in a young architectural practice explained:

> I think that bank managers think women are good at housekeeping so they are probably good at running the books. In the beginning I really dealt with the bank manager, because he actually said, "women are very good with money". Now we've got larger, we have had to split up the responsibilities. My partner deals totally with the financial side of things, I deal totally with marketing. Partly because I'm more of an outgoing personality and like talking to and meeting people and he doesn't.

This notion of distinctive and separate roles for men and women proprietors arose several times in the study. Some female entrepreneurs resent the idea that manufacturing or finance are outside their field of competence. Others work around these beliefs. The potential backer is not disabused of this prejudice, but the women manage the finance or the production. This perception that women are not skilled at managing

Table 3.9   Was security required by lenders?

	Business age		
	<1 year No.	1–5 years No.	>5 years No.
Yes	5	9	7
No	13	21	5
Total	18	30	12

money contrasts with the convention that—in the family business—the money is managed by the wife, while production is the domain of the husband.

Table 3.9 shows the frequency at which security was demanded by lenders. Lack of security and track records were considered to be the major problem for most women; many perceived these to be gender-related difficulties. A partnership running a black model agency described their situation at start-up:

> We got turned down by five or six banks, then we asked a very good friend of ours to borrow £1000 for us. So we took that to the bank and put that down and said well this is what we've got, then we joined Enterprise Allowance. We asked them to loan us a lower amount, we only asked for a quarter of the sum we originally asked for. So we started in December and came up against problems in April . . . we should have started the business with £8000, we only started with £2000.

This response created a situation of double jeopardy for the new business. Without the finance being offered the business could not start. The funds were, however, inadequate. The most common cause of early traumatic failure for new businesses is insufficient start-up capital. Table 3.10 demonstrates that most women believed that start-up would have been easier had more capital been available. Typically, this occurs because the creators of the venture underestimate costs and overestimate earnings. In this fairly common example, their estimates were being cut by the prospective lender.

For this partnership, there was a perception that access to finance was affected by their age, gender and ethnicity.

> A lot of people in the ethnic community come and ask Beverley and me how we started in business. The fact is that we are all so young and the job situation is so bad at the moment that we all want to start a business. But we come from families in council houses, or you're just off the dole or just lost

Table 3.10 In retrospect would starting up have been easier had more capital been available?

	Business age		
	<1 year No.	1–5 years No.	>5 years No.
Yes	13	17	6
No	5	13	6
Total	18	30	12

jobs due to the employment situation. The only problem they face is getting money, the same problem that we faced. When we went to the banks they all said: Oh! brilliant idea but you have no security. So getting money to start up is the major problem. You go to the banks and they say "where's the security?"

The patronizing attitude of bankers towards prospective female entrepreneurs was frequently commented on. Some women realized the need for sympathetic lenders and actively 'shopped around' until they had found a suitable banker. Many respondents cited the need to establish good relationships with bank managers from the outset of the business, although for some this was learnt through experience. Others cited how difficult it was to establish a professional relationship when confronted with patronizing attitudes:

Three of us put £7000 each into the business, we all had to put our houses down as security. With three homes at stake if it all went wrong we looked for two things. First, the right manager, second, low interest rates. We tried three banks before joining the one we're with.

The professionalism of the female entrepreneur can lower barriers to entry. It does seem that there are significant extra costs associated with gender. The more protracted search process consumes time that can be invested in business building. At the same time, shortage of competitive funding alternatives reduces the scope for optimizing the financial package.

Initial problems can be overcome by careful planning and effective controls. The proprietor of a language and marketing training consultancy explained the problems she experienced after 6 months of business ownership:

I think basically I had made the cardinal sin of not going to see my bank manager and not re-doing my business plan. So over the weekend I rewrote the business plan, went to him with the orders that I had. I had quite a lot of orders, well contacts around and potential contacts and suddenly discovered that he was quite human after all. The fact that he had shouted at me over the phone was really because we hadn't met. He had taken over as the new manager. God, this looked to him like an awful company. He said: "look we've got to get this right". Suddenly it was as if somebody had just turned the key, I didn't have to worry about money any more, because I then got this lady in to do the accounts. So she rings me once a week and says right your cash register is this, you have this much in the bank, you owe these bills, you can only pay these . . .

Direct and forceful intervention by this banker was necessary to establish the notion that the banker is a partner in the venture. The business owner's limited experience of working in this way with bankers had introduced a barrier to a productive and effective partnership.

Many women saw the establishment of specialist women-only banks or branches with female lending staff as the only long-term solution to the negative attitudes of bankers (Table 3.11). Over half the respondents said that they thought women-only banks or branches would be useful for female proprietors and almost half stated that they would use a women-only bank if there was one in their vicinity. There are examples of this approach in Britain and elsewhere. The Royal Bank of Scotland has operated a 'women's' branch in Edinburgh for a number of years. There is some evidence that it has a relatively high proportion of women-owned businesses. All the major UK clearing banks have branches with female managers. There are, however, no data on their profile of customers in terms of female-owned businesses. In North America, there are women's banks in New York, California and several other states. It seems that they were especially successful at winning business from new start-ups by women during the late 1970s and early 1980s. A similar pattern can be seen in Scandinavian countries.

Table 3.11　Do you think a 'woman-only' bank is a good idea. If so, would you use one if it was provided locally?

	Good idea		Use bank	
	No.	%	No.	%
Yes	31	52	24	40
No	29	48	36	60
Total	60	100	60	100

Property

In contrast, only 15 respondents experienced problems in finding premises in which to start trading. Twenty-eight respondents started their businesses at home (Table 3.12). This was usually for reasons of convenience and expense. Most of the businesses trading from home were involved in traditionally female activities such as catering. Some did start businesses in new technology-based firms and business consultancy services from home. Trading from home was, for some, a convenient and cautious way into business but it proved to be detrimental to others. These women felt that home-based trading affected their credibility as serious business owners, creating an image of a part-time business for a 'bored housewife with little interest in profits'. The more ambitious, achievement-orientated women expressed this sentiment most strongly.

Home-based working is a useful strategy for respondents with young children. Despite this many state that the presence of young children caused problems. A Glasgow-based business consultant, for instance, although employing a full-time nanny, found it difficult to communicate to her young children that they should not disturb her whilst she was working in her (spare bedroom) office. For women in this sample, benefits of home trading were restricted to clothes and knitwear designers and women undertaking tasks traditionally completed within homes. It did not prove to be a useful strategy for women in new technology-based sectors or with consultancy-based firms.

Very few of the home-based proprietors could look to their spouses for significant support in child care, domestic activities or basic business

Table 3.12 What sort of premises did the business first use to trade?

| | Business age | | |
| | --- | --- | --- |
Concerns	<1 year No.	1–5 years No.	>5 years No.
Home	8	14	6
Shop	0	3	0
Purpose built office	3	4	0
Converted office	1	0	4
Factory	0	5	0
Home/shop	0	1	0
Other	6	3	2
Total	18	30	12

Table 3.13   Did you obtain any help in finding premises?

	Business age		
	<1 year No.	1–5 years No.	>5 years No.
Yes	6	7	2
No	12	23	10
Total	18	30	12

assistance. There were no cases of the spouse taking a lead role in running or managing the home. Few husbands are willing to accept the book-keeper, invoice clerk role conventionally allocated 'to the wife' in male-owned businesses. Passive support allied to financial assistance was the most common type of help given by women to their husband's businesses as reported in other studies (cf. Kirkham, 1987). The now infamous advertisement for Renault depicting a man telling his wife, in the car outside his solicitor's office, that he has mortgaged the house, given up his job, and started a business would take on a different cast if it was his wife making these announcements.

Local authorities were the primary source of help in finding property (Table 3.13). All respondents were eventually able to find premises. Nevertheless, some of the new start businesses experienced problems as a result of a premature move into premises and had subsequent difficulties paying rent. One respondent, a jewellery designer, resolved this by moving the business from the original workshop to her parents' garage. Another, a modelling agency, expressed deep concern about the costs involved and the subsequent effect upon the business. Between the first and second interviews, this particular partnership had left the premises and liquidated the business, unable to cover the overheads.

Advice

The overwhelming majority of the start-ups sought advice on self-employment (Table 3.14). Most undertook training to compensate for any deficiencies of knowledge prior to starting in business. The decision to seek external advice was seen by the women involved as being good business practice and closely linked with future success. There was, however, no evidence that any sources were significantly more linked to success than others. All placed a considerable value on the help they obtained. They regularly returned to this and other sources of business advice. Women business owners seem more willing to seek this initial help and more likely to return for additional counselling than their male counterparts.

A variety of sources of advice about self-employment and business ownership were used. The counselling ranged from formal consultations with bank managers and solicitors to informal conversations with self-employed friends. Some sources were seen as more valuable in all stages of the development of the venture (Table 3.15). Bankers, accountants and local authorities were seen as helpful at all stages. The role of solicitors increased, while that of the Small Firms Service diminished.

Banks and accountants were the major source of advice during the pre-start-up phase. Local enterprise agencies, local authorities and the Small Firms Service had been used by some. Fewer of the more established businesses had approached agencies for advice at the pre-start stage. This may reflect the recent growth of business advisory services. The general advice from agencies was seen to be helpful.

> They kept saying if there is anything else you want to consult me about come back. But a lot of the time I didn't know what it was that I could ask that would help ...

A freelance graphic artist found general small business advisory services useful but limited. There are some indications that dedicated, specialist agencies are seen as being more useful. The technical ability and knowledge of specialist agencies dealing with creative products, such as knitwear and jewellery design, proved to be very welcome. This graphic artist turned to the comprehensive counselling which was given by an agency specializing in business advice for artists and designers.

> ... Whereas as soon as I went to the Creative Training Company they suddenly gave me a whole lot of information that was helpful. They also

Table 3.14   Stages at which advice or information was sought.

	Business age		
Concerns	<1 year No.	1–5 years No.	>5 years No.
Pre-start-up	16	20	6
Start-up	13	23	7
Ongoing	8	19	9

Table 3.15   From whom did you receive HELPFUL advice when starting up?

	Business age		
Concerns	<1 year No.	1–5 years No.	>5 years No.
Bank	5	4	4
Solicitor	0	6	3
Accountant	6	10	4
Family	0	3	1
Friends	3	4	2
Job Centre	2	0	1
Previous employer	0	0	0
Local authority	2	2	1
Small Firms Service	1	1	0
Local enterprise agency	0	5	1
Trade Association	0	0	1
Citizens' Advice Bureau	0	1	0
More than three above	4	5	1
None of above	7	3	2
Other	0	1	0
Instances	30	45	21

Table 3.16   From whom did you receive UNHELPFUL advice when starting up?

	Business age		
Concerns	<1 year No.	1–5 years No.	>5 years No.
Bank	1	7	4
Solicitor	1	0	1
Accountant	0	5	1
Local authority	0	2	0
Instances	2	14	6

started offering me more advice, I had put the other problems that were there to them and they started to show me ways to get round them.

There was a high level of dissatisfaction with the commercial services provided by banks, solicitors and accountants during the start-up period. Twenty respondents who had approached these professional organizations for assistance found them to be unhelpful (Table 3.16). For some women, there was a belief that some professionals were not able to counsel smaller businesses effectively. A London-based food manufacturer explained:

> He wasn't orientated to small businesses and his attitude wasn't good. Rather than help me to do things like my business plans and cash flow, he wanted me to go away and do it, so that I could take it back to him and he could check it. He didn't really give me help as such.

Other women also perceived a lack of understanding of the particular problems of small businesses:

> I think you really have to make decisions yourself in what suits your business. I think that a lot of people who try to give you help think you have thousands of people working in an office or factory. Big accountants that don't know anything about small business. We had a consultant that was an awful lot of help in some respects, but he expected you to have about four staff who could do the paper work, get figures, which you haven't got time for.

The pattern of these responses raises important issues about the nature of the support provided during crucial stages in the evolution of the enterprise. Banks and accountants seem to be at their most effective during the start-up and maturity phase in the life of the business. They appear to be less effective at helping these businesses during the turbulent years of business development. These early years see the highest rates of business failure and withdrawal for all types of venture.

For other women, dissatisfaction with professional services was attributable to gender-related factors. The same patronizing attitudes which confronted them when raising finance were present when seeking general advice from bankers and accountants. Many respondents stated that their personal ability to manage the venture was continually being questioned. The choice of female accountants was seen as an especially effective tactic to overcome these problems and was adopted by a large proportion of the proprietors. Those adopting this approach often had difficulty in finding female bank managers.

Few women expressed a need for single-sex advisory agencies, such as local enterprise agencies. They were more concerned that specialist sectoral as well as general advice was available from these sources. There was a perception, however, that female counselling staff within local enterprise agencies were an invaluable source of support. Despite the emphasis on sectoral or technical help there was little use of the more obvious sources of this help: trade associations, industry research associations, educational institutions or Chambers of Commerce. Women were

Table 3.17 Who do business owners turn to when decision making?*

Source of advice	Daily decisions	%	Major decisions	%
Friends, family	36	60	23	38
Business partner	23	38	24	40
Staff	9	15	3	5
Consultants	19	33	25	42
Lawyers, banks or accountants	21	35	33	56
Yourself	28	47	19	32

* Multiple responses permitted.

either ignorant of this help or found difficulty gaining their assistance during the start-up phase of their venture.

Advice for the small business beyond the immediate start-up period proved to be even harder to find. Several of the respondents with more established businesses expressed problems in finding suitable advisors. Perhaps as a reaction to this, most women turned to either friends or family if they needed any help in daily decision making, using professional advisors only in major decision making (Table 3.17).

One manufacturer expressed the need for guidance for the ongoing small business:

> I wish there was some government body that I could go to and say, "look, this is the situation I'm in and I need help. Where can I get someone in marketing? Where can I get this kind of person?" I don't feel that there is anything, I tried the MSC [Manpower Services Commission]. I know that I could get somebody to fulfil a particular function, but I would have to know what function I wanted that person to do. At the moment I'm in a different situation, I need someone to talk over the options, the variables. I need advice and guidance really.

The Enterprise Initiative had not reached this group. The predominant image of maleness portrayed in the advertising of this Initiative may have an affect on the rate of usage by female entrepreneurs.

For women with established businesses, advice is sought as much to offset the loneliness of sole ownership as a need for professional guidance. One respondent, passing on advice to women with newer businesses, said:

> I would advise people starting in business to make sure that they are very well grounded in the legal basics. If that means taking advice from professional people, then you should do so. That includes very basic things like making sure you are properly insured, covering all the ground work thoroughly. Once you've done the ground work and made the product

saleable, it's no longer a matter of advice, but confidence and a belief in yourself that you can do it.

As we have seen, the women surveyed in this study demonstrate the growing awareness of the value of business planning. For women, the need to plan reflects not only a practical need for all business start-ups, but also a way of compensating for doubts about their personal ability in running and managing a business. Often as a result of extensive planning, successful women had largely managed to put together the package of resources required for business start-up. This was often achieved in the face of adversity.

CASE STUDY

Company activity:	*Data Processing*
Company started:	*1986*
Employees:	*16*
Business organization:	*Limited Company*

Company History

To be free, to take the risk is almost like painting a picture. It's creating something which I think has got some art in it. It is setting things in place, and seeing them grow. You are able to put your own ideas into practice. They don't all work. Rather than that, it's a creative activity.

This respondent had founded and runs one of the largest, and fastest growing data processing companies in Scotland. Although the business has only been trading for a short time, since April 1986, it is expected to turn over £250 000 during the next financial year. Its current workforce of 16 employees is planned to increase by a third during the early part of 1988.

The respondent started her business when in her late forties, after holding a number of senior management positions in nursing management and corporate planning. She returned to Britain from Iran after the revolution as a single parent with two children, and virtually no capital or possessions.

The respondent returned to university to study for a postgraduate management qualification (an MBA) before joining a large oil company as a corporate planner. After 5 years she was made redundant during an organizational restructure, although the respondent believes this was influenced by a period of ill health she had suffered immediately prior to her redundancy. She had, however, been planning a move into self-employment for some time and had organized her business before being made redundant. Through a number of profitable ventures into property purchase and renovation, and by taking advantage of the capital gains tax laws, the respondent had built up a substantial personal income.

Start Up

The respondent maintains that poor treatment by her previous employer, both in terms of status and pay, was one of her prime motivators for self-employment. Business ownership, the respondent believes, allows her to take control of her 'life destiny', in contrast to her position while working for larger organizations.

In practical terms, however, the respondent has been meticulous in the planning and development of her business. The capital built up through property renovation provided the whole £25 000 required to set up the data processing business. By providing all the initial finance herself, the respondent avoided dealing with financial institutions; she recognizes that she would encounter problems convincing anyone that a woman is capable of being successful in this area. Overheads were kept to a minimum as the company initially traded from the respondent's home and careful selection and planning preceded the recent purchase of newly refitted premises. These offices have been chosen for the opportunities they offer for expansion and the respondent estimates that the amount of work being done there can increase threefold before new premises become necessary.

Although the respondent has had a number of years management experience, she was unsure of her ability to deal with her staff on a 'face to face' basis:

> It is difficult, I think, especially for me since I have not been used to dealing with what I call shop floor level. I had to modify my behaviour and change my sort of level of communication. So, I tend to talk more through my data prep manager. Although I keep in close contact with the girls, there are certain things I need translated for me.

Central to the respondent's management style is the provision of a good working environment for her staff. Her reasons for this are not altogether altruistic as the respondent is aware of the need to develop a stable and reliable workforce in an industry where skilled data processors are in demand. Given poor pay and conditions offered by her rivals, the respondent feels confident that her strategy will be successful.

The respondent relies on her data preparation manager for much of personnel and training needs. This woman was her first employee and has played an integral role in the set up and subsequent growth of the business. She deals with the day-to-day running of the business, leaving the respondent free to concentrate on developing marketing strategies and client networks. Despite the respondent's success in this area, she believes that, as a woman, she is at a disadvantage in developing contracts and securing orders for a number of reasons. She cannot call on the 'old boy network' used by many of her competitors to secure orders. By developing her own contacts and through her growing reputation for reliability and efficiency, the respondent is gradually building her own client network to combat more traditional structures. A second difficulty encountered in developing client relationships has involved the entertainment of potential clients. As a single woman the respondent feels uncomfortable about inviting male clients for lunch or dinner. In order to counteract this, the respondent has organized a series of open days where potential customers can come to her premises and meet her 'on her own ground'.

Growth and Development

Between the first and second interviews, the respondent was successful in securing contracts which will keep her business working at full capacity for the near future. She took her success in this as a signal to expand. She has developed closer relations with the multinational company from which she leases her equipment, and has negotiated favourable arrangements for the leasing of more new equipment. This will enable her to take on larger orders, expanding into the presently underutilized areas of her premises.

By attending a conference in London, the respondent's ideas about the data processing industry were confirmed, reinforcing her confidence in the future of her company, and in the markets in which it operates:

> Because of the view that it was a declining market, many business have actually gone out of business, but I saw the need that there was still a market, but it was a changed market. Much more professional, with a lot more capital investment in training and so on. The whole business had to be professional. It was a different environment and thankfully, my tactics and marketing have proven to be correct.

This respondent's business is growing rapidly. Yet, it is growing within a predefined framework developed by the respondent before the business was set up. At each stage of business development the respondent has utilized her experience in the management of change to guide her company along her chosen lines. This has not, however, resulted in an inflexible approach to business development. On the contrary, the respondent emphasized the need for flexibility:

> The market keeps changing. When you are setting up and running a business like this, you have got to be flexible and change to grow with your business or you will be stranded.

Where she has been unsure of particular areas, as in employee relations, she has bought in the necessary skills. Throughout the life of the business, the respondent's need for control has not limited growth, as her experience in management has provided her with the ability to delegate day-to-day decision making where necessary. A clue to the respondent's approach to control and delegation may be found in her views on what constitutes control over her environment:

> I don't think it's power. I think it is freedom more than power. If you have money you have power and so on. Freedom and control over the environment, which includes job, but that is only one of them. There are a lot more. Frankly, I got fed up of telling other people what to do all the time, and how to compromise my own ideas, imagination and so forth, and I just got quite sick of it.

The respondent does not see business ownership simply as a means of gaining control of her working environment. Through becoming a successful and prosperous business owner she hopes to gain freedom over all aspects of her life. Another strand to the respondent's objectives involves her beliefs about how women in business are treated:

> I am not a feminist, don't think for one minute. The majority of businesses are set up to suit male methods of working, which is quite different from females. Females are much more down to earth and practical. I can't be bothered with the politics. Men spend more time in an organization watching their backs, making sure they are in the right position . . .

The respondent emphasizes her wish to create a female orientated environment for her almost exclusively female staff, with flexible arrangements for domestic crisis, school holidays etc. On a more personal level she sees a successful business as a means of creating a more rewarding environment for herself.

4

Enterprise in Action: The Problems Women Experience When Running Their Businesses

Women owning and managing enterprises face some distinctive and some general (non-gender) problems. Most businesses had been in existence for less than 2 years, but there is a significant subset of much older firms. The general perspective is of comparatively new businesses. Distinct differences do appear between newer businesses and those in existence for more than 5 years. Analysis by sector and by firm size also brings out additional differences in the types of problems affecting the owner-manager and the ways in which these problems are handled.

The richness of the qualitative data gathered from these entrepreneurs and the challenges they faced must be counterbalanced by a recognition of the problems researchers have when relying upon verbal reports and individual explanations to investigate prior or current experience. There are potential problems concerning the accuracy of retrospective recall. There are, especially in the case of small business research, difficulties in distinguishing 'perceived problems' from 'real problems'. Gender-based research is no exception; the previous social and political experiences of the interviewees often determine whether discrimination is perceived and recognized as such. In other instances, the interview itself may be a determining factor; by probing and encouraging the interviewee to discuss her experiences in terms of gender, the interviewer may raise the level of consciousness and recognition of gender discrimination among the sample.

Many interviewees in this study asserted that they were not feminists and, moreover, appeared hostile to that philosophy. As one interviewee said:

> I'm not a women's libber or anything like that and I don't get on my high horse about it. I'm just doing my job like anybody else. I just happen to be a woman.

This fit between a conventional 'world view' and a non-conventional 'lifestyle' poses problems of cognitive dissonance for these entrepreneurs. Generally, they resolve this by placing a premium on personal achievement. In contrast, a significant minority (40%) did believe that aspects of business ownership are harder for female entrepreneurs, often despite their inability to identify specific areas in which discrimination existed. Some overarching explanations were given spontaneously. The lack of any previous opportunity to develop business skills and knowledge was often given as the key difference. As is noted in Chapter 1, this awareness of gender differences among the self-employed and entrepreneurs may, in part, be a function of two particular factors. First, there is the general awareness of the constraints on labour force participation of women in the overall economy. Second, their direct experience of gender discrimination as self-employed women led them to recognize specific challenges.

The difference between perceived barriers and real problems is central to this study, but is difficult to isolate and address quantitatively. This issue poses special problems to any attempt to attribute specific problems to gender. In order to overcome this methodological difficulty, the writers have taken a pragmatic approach to the comments and sentiments of the female entrepreneurs. Where empirical evidence to support statements is available it is noted. Elsewhere the respondents' own words determine our comments.

The major questions addressed by this study are:

(1) Do problems commonly associated with business ownership have a gender dimension?

(2) Does gender exacerbate the normal problems of business formation?

(3) Do women face additional gender-related problems which do not affect male business owners?

The first question is harder to isolate and address quantitatively. Many of the challenges of business formation are common to all business owners. Often they are an inevitable outcome of the desire to persuade others to share the entrepreneur's risk. A third party cannot be expected to take at face value the visions and aspirations of the innovator. The barriers to start-up are important aspects of the process of weaning out weak ideas and poor proposals. Normally, it is better not to start in business than to fail catastrophically.

It is difficult to establish the extent to which these barriers are increased by gender. Some problems, such as childcare provision and domestic

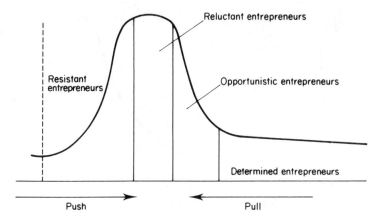

Figure 4.1 The entrepreneurial curve.

support, have a clear gender dimension. A more insidious gender dimension may, however, affect women in other aspects of business. The gender of the business owner may affect the payment policies of customers. Many female proprietors report that they lack skills in debt collection. Sometimes they feel they are less assertive than their male counterparts. Some women may interpret this as a problem exacerbated by gender. Others may see it as a variation on the more general theme of enterprise aspirations which can be summarized in terms of the entrepreneurial curve (Fig. 4.1).

The entrepreneurial curve gives a valuable insight into the profile of the entrepreneurial population. Higher barriers to enterprise will deter different groups.

'Determined' entrepreneurs are the smallest group in the population. Their resolve enables them to overcome difficulties which deter the majority of those with aspirations to business ownership.

'Opportunistic' entrepreneurs are a larger group. They will become business owners to exploit a specific opening or series of opportunities. They can be deterred by risks which seem to outweigh the economic or personal gains from the venture. Temporary setbacks which reduce the scope for success can prevent start-up. Both these groups are 'pulled' into entrepreneurial behaviour by opportunities.

'Reluctant' entrepreneurs will include self-employment as an avenue to develop in the face of adversity. They might develop a venture if it offers improved prospects when unemployed. Inheritors of businesses commonly show these signs of reluctance. 'Resistant' entrepreneurs will only consider starting a business in extreme circumstances. They with-

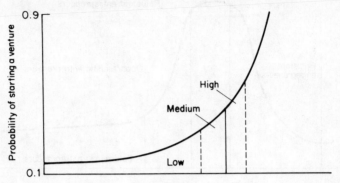

Figure 4.2   Barriers to business development.

draw or cease trading at the first opportunity. These two groups are 'pushed' into self-employment.

All the women in this study fell into one of these bands. The more successful fell into the first two categories. These are the groups most likely to be encouraged by positive action by support agencies. Favourable or unpleasant experiences can affect the location of individual entrepreneurs. A 'reluctant' entrepreneur can become 'opportunistic' if personal enterprise becomes associated with individual benefit. This increases the probability that she will start a venture and strive to overcome barriers to entry (Fig. 4.2).

The issue of whether gender exacerbates business problems is further complicated when examining the management strategies adopted by women in dealing with problems. A successful strategy implies that the problem is either controlled, resolved temporarily or disappears altogether. In these cases, the issue is whether they can be interpreted as problems at all. The women were asked to define for themselves where the problem areas lay and whether they felt them to be gender related. Problems identified by the respondents ranged from the technical and operational issues of business ownership, to the more personal issues, notably the effect of business ownership upon domestic lives. A substantial minority (40%) of respondents were unequivocal in their belief that self-employment and business ownership is harder for women than men. Forty per cent also stated that the business problems were made worse because of their gender.

In Table 4.1 we look at some of the most commonly cited problem areas and how they affect the business owners. The most common problem, and the one cited as being the most problematic of all, was the delayed

Table 4.1 Common problems in running the business.*

	Any problems		Most serious	
	No.	%†	No.	%‡
Late payment of bills	35	58	19	32
Undercharging	30	50	6	10
Cash flow problems	24	40	9	15
Employing staff	20	33	6	10
Effect on personal circumstances	20	33	3	5
Getting business/finding clients	19	32	7	12
VAT on unpaid bills	16	27	1	2
Finding premises	15	25	2	3
Marketing	15	25	1	2
Book-keeping	14	23	1	2
Taxation issues	14	23	1	2
Property insurance	10	17	0	0
Getting advice	9	15	1	2
National insurance	7	12	0	0
Laws/regulations	6	10	1	2
Form filling	6	10	0	0
No problems	2	3	2	3

* Seventeen possible problem areas.
† Percentage of those who answered 'yes' for each category of problem, multiple answers possible.
‡ Most important problem only noted. One response per person over all 17 categories.

payment of bills by customers. Not only was it the most common problem, it was also the most intractable. Other problems mentioned were undercharging for a product or service, difficulties in cash flow management, managing and retaining staff, getting business and finding clients and the effect of business ownership upon personal circumstances. This last problem area proved to be so complex and evoked such differing responses that it is discussed separately in Chapter 8. The five most frequently mentioned problems illustrate how operational problems which affect all business owners are sometimes perceived as having a gender dimension. The same issues consequently may affect female proprietors differently to males in the same situation (Table 4.2). Three of the five areas relate to the financial base and management of the companies. They may stem from an initial under-capitalization of the business. They are not wholly connected to employment problems and difficulties in recruiting customers. The way these topics are viewed is affected by the respondent's perceptions of gender-related issues.

Table 4.2   Are problems exacerbated or
made easier because you are a
woman?

	No.
Exacerbated	24
Eased	0
No difference	36
Total	60

Finance

The late payment of bills by customers and clients was the most commonly cited problem. Over half the respondents cited this as a problem area. Almost a third stated that this was their greatest difficulty. Previous studies of small business owner managers have highlighted this area as being a major source of recurrent difficulties for the small business proprietor. Many respondents in this study expressed the view that getting paid was as difficult for men as for women. A significant minority believed that for women, the problem is more difficult to resolve.

The gender dimension appeared to be manifested in their lack of commercial experience and an associated lack of confidence and assertiveness which inhibited the respondents in following up bad debts and pressing for payment. The owner of an alternative health practice described the problem:

> ... its just trying to get the money out of them—that's very difficult in some cases and you have to be very careful because they are customers. Okay, they are not very good payers but we do need their custom as well. It's a very fine dividing line between how ruthless and rude you should be with the buyers yet can still get the money out of them.

The personalizing of commercial relations is a characteristic of many small business owners. The less successful business owners lack the business skills and experience to set up and implement formal and systematic approaches to debt management. Younger women and women in newer businesses were particularly affected by this. Often their enterprises ran on small and tight budgets. They were less able to cope with late payment of accounts than either older respondents or those with more established businesses.

The joint owner of a first aid supplies business stated:

> We didn't realize we would sell the original £2000 worth of stock in a month. We had to replace our £2000 stock when the bills were coming in, but the people weren't paying in the 28 days that they were meant to pay. But we

never saw this at the time so we ended up running about £1000 behind all the time.

The combination of inadequate prior research and optimistic assumptions about payment led this firm to undercharge and face grave cash flow problems. Women running more established businesses had fewer problems with delayed payment, suggesting that there is a noticeable learning curve. Over time, these women develop skills and confidence to manage their payment and debt collection systems. The co-owner of a clothes manufacturing firm took pride in the fact that the company had never used an overdraft facility despite recurrent problems with late payments:

We still haven't gone into the red yet, we are staying in the black at the bank. We were moaning this morning that we have got about eight or nine thousand owing to us, which is a lot of money. But I was saying to Ken this morning, 6 months ago we couldn't even afforded to have been outstanding three thousand, so we must be making a lot of progress. We would have been climbing up the walls if someone owed us three thousand 6 months ago.

One respondent, working in stained glass design and manufacture, found that even grants for business could cause cash flow problems if they were delayed:

Concerning cash flow, one of the biggest problems has been that we are waiting for grants to come in and they can take a long time to process at the moment, particularly the regional development grants. Or, you have actually got to spend the money before you can reclaim it.

Undercharging for products and services was a major concern for the women interviewed. Two main reasons were highlighted. Firstly, many small companies, such as those interviewed, operate in specialist areas. This avoids the need to compete with other companies but can create difficulties in establishing reference points for pricing decisions. A retailer specializing in lace products explained:

It's something that people have been out of the way of buying for a long time . . . and they are totally unaware of what the price—a standard price— should be. They can't compare our stuff with anything in another shop.

This experience may be typical of small companies which attempt to develop new markets and break into specialist sectors. Secondly, as women are often drawn into specialist markets through a lack of saleable skills, they are particularly susceptible to problems associated with 'breaking new ground' in terms of market and demand. In support of this, women operating in traditionally female sectors appear to be less affected by poor pricing policies. A two-woman partnership who recently started a private language school described their experiences of undercharging having completed their first year of business:

> It's not just like passing off a few commodities and working out what it costs. I think what happened is we ended up giving an excellent service, we had super feedback, I think we got the balance right on both the education side and the jamboree, have fun side and outings and sports. We did seem to have got the balance right. The only thing we didn't get right was the price.
>
> It's urgent, we need organizing from a financial point of view. We didn't make a profit this summer, which is sad, really sad, because we had more students than we expected, we worked around the clock. Had we charged more, ten pounds extra, we would have been okay. But these are all things that people should know about before they go into business. We thought as we were new, we should be highly competitive, and we gave the lowest price and it was foolish. We didn't handle the business as such, it was difficult to realize that education doesn't come free, we have a commodity and it has to be run as a business.

The failure to properly charge for time and understate overheads is typical of ventures operated by those with little business experience. It is possible that those women whose time and work is undervalued by others will undervalue their own time. Undercharging is linked with both the limited business experience and a general lack of confidence the respondents displayed as business owners. This prompted many women to use low prices as a market entry strategy. They sometimes showed a surprising lack of confidence in both their product and their business skills. Pricing was largely undertaken on a cost plus basis. This was an especially dangerous policy for those who lacked skills in properly estimating costs. Others use price as an effective, if risky, market entry device. A partner from a first aid supplies business explained her situation:

> I don't think anyone could have helped price it. Because we knew the kind of prices we were dealing with already. We were trying to undercut too much. You know, we were trying to make a big impact. But I don't think it was necessary to undercut as much as we did. Now, our prices are fair and they are still a good bit cheaper than our competitors.

A graphic designer had a similar outlook but viewed the risks in a more calculated way:

> There are a lot of things I have underpriced. But you have got to get yourself into the market. I'm used by a big London publicity company which is one

of the biggest in London because I'm cheap and I'm quick and I'll work through the night. Next year I'm not going to be so cheap. But I've got to get the job and I know, more or less, what type of thing to expect and I know what I'm capable of. I had to get into business and maybe make a loss with it.

Buying entry into a market in this way puts considerable pressure on the financial resources of the venture. Unexpected financial demands, delays in developing a mature market or some other unexpected circumstances can lead to failure. The effect of both undercharging and delayed payment of bills on the businesses was dangerous. Many experienced serious cash flow management problems as a consequence. Forty per cent of the sample cited cash flow management as a problem area and 15% stated that it was the area of greatest difficulty. Often these problems of cash flow management were related to initial under-capitalization of the business. There was a wide variation in the amounts of capital used in starting businesses. Many were seriously under-capitalized. Several women made these problems worse by cautious borrowing. The following quotes illustrate this attitude:

> We are both married and both got mortgages and if we take on too much we are kind of frightened that it all collapses round about us and then we have got to leave our houses, etc. etc. That kind of puts us off a bit. Whereas you see men in business, they have to make a livelihood for their families, but they seem to go deeper into debt to make money to get things quicker.

> When we started in business 3 years ago we got £2000 from the Local Enterprise Agency. We could have got £3000 at the time, but we thought, its too much to pay back if anything goes wrong.

A graphic designer in the process of starting up echoed these sentiments:

> I think my main worry is that I am not going to be able to set up if I don't get the money. If I do get the money and borrow from the bank I worry that I am not going to pay it back fast enough . . . but I do worry that I would let people down in the beginning who lend me money and also my husband is worried whether or not it will be a success.

The preoccupation with repayment rather than business development reflects a reluctance to risk family assets for the business. While cautious borrowing influenced many women, others were simply unable to raise the amount needed from institutional sources. Lack of security and financial and credit track records were major problems for most women, many of whom saw these difficulties as gender related. A partnership of two women operating a black model agency reduced borrowing requirements but were left under-capitalized:

> I'm living on the poverty line. I may not look it, but I have to look this way to go to work, but within myself I know that I am living on the poverty line. It wouldn't be like this now if we had invested more in the business... it wouldn't be like this because we would be able to take a wage and not worry about going into money which was there for a good reason. We can't take any drawings because that money has got to be used to pay bills or to do something else within the business.

Another respondent commented:

> The biggest barrier is money, lack of money. Until we have got the money or can afford to do more marketing, we can't really whack up our turnover much.

Few of the newer businesses were able to achieve the growth desired by the proprietor within the first 2 years. Lack of start-up capital is the single, largest constraint on early growth. It prevents investment in new machinery, it restricts marketing investments and it makes recruitment of new staff impossible.

Older businesses, most of which operated in non-traditionally female sectors such as light engineering and manufacturing, had invested heavily at start-up, and suffered fewer problems. These proprietors demonstrated an ability to access ongoing and growth capital and a subsequent greater rate of growth. The owner of a wire manufacturing company stated:

> To be honest, if I wasn't able to shop around and deal with bank managers, I'd be a pretty pathetic business owner.

Credibility

This professional and instrumental view was a key feature in the strategies adopted by the more successful proprietors. Once start-up problems are resolved, usually at start-up, female proprietors have few problems with recurrent finance. Difficulties seem to occur at certain key transitional stages: the move from part- to full-time ownership; the start-up; the move to a new market requiring large capital inputs. Credibility with external support agencies and intermediaries appears to be important in overcoming these challenges and managing change or transition successfully. Most women felt strongly that many of the problems of credibility were gender related.

A consultant specializing in financial services and advice for women, who had invested £50 000 at start-up and now employed 62 people, passed on the following advice:

> I would advise a woman starting in business to make sure that she was not under-capitalized in the first place. Under-capitalization can be a great source of stress. I would make sure that she was opening up a business in a field she knew. Not to be starry eyed about thinking there was some long shot that she was going to fulfil. Then, to produce a business plan, to go over it with her lawyer and accountant. If she had a friendly bank manager, show him. Generally speaking, be realistic and down to earth about it.

Employing Others

Employing people is the area of greatest concern for one in ten firms and an area of major concern for all others. Causes of anxiety varied between the recruitment and retention of appropriate staff to the development of employer–employee relationships. Many of the women interviewed expressed problems of recruitment common to all small businesses. The owner of a pharmaceutical manufacturing plant stated:

> The main problem is that most reps want a car with their job, and we, being a small company, can't afford to give them a car, so this is the whole difficulty.

Others found that their main recruitment problems lay in a shortage of skilled labour. Difficulties of employing skilled machinists for textile manufacturing in Nottingham were emphasized by all the respondents concerned with this sector.

> It would be nice to expand, but, as I say, the main problem at the moment is to get the people to do the job. It seems ridiculous and the same story over and over again, but it really is quite a problem. Whether it will get better next year, I just don't know, but it makes you apprehensive about expansion. As I say, I have taken on more lines this season and I have found that it has not gone the way that it should have gone, because I just cannot get the people to do the job.

Problems with recruitment have had an impact upon the management style adopted by this company:

> Obviously you are going to get disappointed by certain people, but I still feel that the majority of people are good. If you try and work in a friendly atmosphere and you get the work done, it is the only way to be. I think it is the only way we can be at the moment, you can't wield the whip at them

because they know the position—they can just get up and go across the road to someone else.

Respondents were asked a series of questions regarding their criteria for employee recruitment and the preferences they harboured for staff characteristics (Table 4.3). The majority of women expressed a preference for specific skills relating to their business sector. Half the respondents preferred employees to have had previous work experience, although three interviewees specifically recruited school leavers as "they haven't had a chance to develop bad habits". These comments are typical of those heard from all types of business owners.

Employing Women

A striking feature of the women in the study was their preference for employing other women. Over a third of the respondents state a preference for employing women. This compares to only two respondents who preferred to employ men. Preference for female employees was based on both pragmatic, personal and managerial reasons. This prevalence of female employees often reflected the type of jobs created by the firms. It was, however, just as likely to occur where there was no obvious sex bias in the employment profile of the sector. There was also a widely held belief that female employees were more adaptable, worked harder and were less likely to challenge the authority of the proprietor.

Table 4.3 Preference of staff characteristics.

| | Preference* | | | | | |
| | Yes | | No | | Not important | |
Criteria for employment	No.	%	No.	%	No.	%
Specific skills	43	72	3	5	10	17
Work experience	29	48	3	5	24	40
Women returning to work	23	38	1	2	32	53
Sex preference—female	21	35	0	0	33	55
Qualifications	18	30	8	13	30	50
Other preferences	8	13	47	78	1	2
Marital status—single	3	5	0	0	51	85
Marital status—married	2	3	0	0	51	85
Sex preference—male	2	3	0	0	33	55

*Multiple responses given.

The owner of a data processing company attributed her preference for female employees to her experience working in a multinational company:

> I am not a feminist, don't think for one minute, but the majority of businesses are set up to suit male methods of working, which is quite different from females. Females are much more down to earth and practical. I can't be bothered with the politics, men spend more time in an organiz- ation watching their backs, making sure they are in the right position.

Another compared her male and female apprentices:

> The boy has recently arrived and already there are some differences that are quite marked. There have been some difficulties already. He's fairly okay and we made it quite clear at the beginning that he washes the cups the same as everybody else, but there are things he doesn't seem to do that the girls do. The cleaning seems to take him forever. You know, there are things like that . . .

Some women suggested that male employees were unwilling to take instructions from them and mostly dealt with this by channelling re- quests through a male manager or supervisor or, in two cases, through male domestic partners. Many respondents expressed a preference for employing women returning to work after a period outside employment. These women were seen as 'more reliable', especially if they had older and more independent children. Generally, respondents were suppor- tive of women returning to the labour market, although the marital status of staff was not a major issue for them. There was a slight preference among those in traditionally female areas in favour of women returning to work and female employees.

Not all respondents gave their unconditional support to women with children returning to work.

> I have deep misgivings about women going to work soon after having babies. I worry tremendously about the first 2 years of a child's life. I have done quite a lot of reading about it, and having had children, I think it is really sad, that there is no parent there.

Skills

The most pronounced divisions in the responses regarding recruitment preferences were between women operating businesses in the new sectors and those in non-traditional and traditional sectors (Table 4.4). Business owners in the new sectors emphasized the need for previous work experience and specific skills, reflecting the technology base of many of these businesses. Specialist skills were less in demand in the non-traditional sectors.

Several women emphasized the need for a 'flexible' workforce for small businesses, echoing their preference for 'more adaptable' female employees. Some respondents emphasized the need for careful selection of employees for all small businesses, believing that one unsuitable

Table 4.4   Criteria upon which staff are recruited (cross-sectional comparison).

Criteria/sector	Yes	%	No	%	Not important	%
Females						
Non-traditional	6	33	0	0	11	60
New sector	5	33	0	0	9	60
Traditional	10	43	0	0	13	56
Males						
Non-traditional	1	6	0	0	11	60
New sector	1	7	0	0	9	60
Traditional	0	0	0	0	13	56
Work experience						
Non-traditional	7	39	1	8	10	36
New sector	13	87	1	7	1	7
Traditional	9	39	1	4	13	56
Qualifications						
Non-traditional	8	44	1	6	9	50
New sector	8	53	2	13	5	33
Traditional	2	9	5	22	16	70
Specific skills						
Non-traditional	11	61	2	11	5	28
New sector	14	93	0	0	1	7
Traditional	18	78	1	4	4	17
Women returning to work						
Non-traditional	5	28	0	0	13	72
New sector	9	60	0	0	6	40
Traditional	9	39	1	4	13	56
Single people						
Non-traditional	1	6	0	0	17	94
New sector	0	0	0	0	15	100
Traditional	2	9	0	0	19	83
Married people						
Non-traditional	0	0	0	0	17	94
New sector	0	0	0	0	15	100
Traditional	2	9	0	0	19	83

employee would have a detrimental impact on the performance of the company as a whole and, with resources scarce, be costly to replace. This people orientation seems to occur more often in research among women owner managers than in earlier, non-gender-specific research. This, however, might be a factor of time. The recent emphasis on the better use of human resources for competitive advantage might influence views.

Women whose businesses operated in sectors which employed skilled staff expressed greatest concern about both recruitment and retention. Some businesses deliberately held extensive staff training programmes to cope with skill shortages. Many felt, however, that they had special problems in retaining staff and were willing to experiment with different forms of business organization in an attempt to overcome this problem.

> Another big barrier we came across was getting staff. The way we overcame that is we got unskilled people and we trained them. Once again that uses up a lot of money. . . . The next main problem was keeping the people you have trained. We have spent so much on training people and keeping people, and the way you do that is to make sure that we get more profitable so they can earn good money. Then we will try profit sharing or even make the company into a co-operative. Otherwise they will leave. I mean they really will. You can't keep people unless the company is really worth it.

Maternalism

Employer–employee relationships posed further problems for the respondents. The development of effective management styles, explored more fully in Chapter 5, was an important step in coping with these issues. A maternalistic style, characterized by a unitaristic view of employee relations, was a very successful policy. It was frequently adopted by older, more experienced women. Employees, especially females, were seen as being part of a family. The owner of a pharmaceutical manufacturing plant:

> I go to every meeting and I like to think that all the girls know that I would never ever ask them to do anything that I couldn't do and they know that I started at the bottom, like them, and have worked my way up. They know that they could ask me anything and I'd be able to tell them. I haven't just come in at a management level, I've actually worked my way up, they know that this is the case and I suppose that I've got a good relationship with them all.

> The reason we are so lucky is because it is a bit like an extended family. Any woman in this organization, family or not, would have the same adjustment

as anyone else. We have had children at various times, sitting around drawing with crayons . . . so we tend to work a little more flexibly.

As in paternalist ownership, authority and control lie firmly with the owner. One woman, having proudly described the family atmosphere of her firm, later in the interview stated "when I say jump, they jump". Other 'matriarchs' also remarked:

> I know sometimes they think I have got an acid tongue. When they come in to see me with messages I'll say things like, I hope that's not gum you are chewing, and they'll say, "Well, yes, it is gum actually". I'll say, "Go outside and take that out of your mouth!" like a headmistress. Because if you have ideas of becoming a secretary, let me tell you now, you don't carry on like that.

> Well at the end of the day, you don't let pity or anything come into it, because if they are pulling you down they could lose you the work and at the end of the day that work is your business and your money. I have become a lot harder, in fact, I'd say I've changed immensely over the last 3 years. I used to be known as quite soft, but I'm very hard when somebody is messing me around. They know that if they do a good job they'll get rewarded but mess me around and they'll certainly know.

In contrast some younger respondents stated that they felt awkward about their role as employers.

> Being an employer, a role I understand very well, at the same time it has brought me directly into conflict with elements within myself. For me, personally, how people get on in the office is fundamental because it affects me so badly if they don't. That is quite a big stress point for me. If I find someone working against me, for whatever reason, I like to bring it out into the open, sort it out. I have found that very difficult in the past.

> I found dealing with employees quite easy on the one hand and on the other difficult. I had a lot to learn. It is like developing a rather cynical edge, without being cynical, maybe looking a bit beyond just their CV and what they say to you at the interview. It has been difficult developing a relationship on a friendly level and then having to discipline them in some way. I have done a number of courses which have been remarkably supportive and educational in that area.

Working Through Others

Young women, inexperienced in management and lacking the age to develop a credible management style, struggled most. One respondent referred to an assumed competence, which tends to be attributed to most men, but not to most women. A number of other women described similar feelings. Some women suggested that they had to earn credibility, not just with their business colleagues and customers, but also with their employees. One woman deals with her lack of experience by employing a staff supervisor through whom she can channel requests.

> When she is away I have the problems of the whole office on my shoulders and worrying about the girls and keeping them occupied and I've got my own work to do, so we tend to have a very friendly relationship with the staff. I'm not saying that's bad, but on the other hand I think that one should have a certain amount of distance, not a lot but a certain amount. Sometimes if its too familiar, then people become a little too easy going. There isn't the amount of discipline there ought to be.

Recruiting Customers

Getting business and finding clients was frequently put forward as a recurrent practical problem. Greatest difficulty appeared to be experienced within the new and emerging sectors. Almost half of these respondents highlight problems in this area. By contrast, only one in five of respondents operating in non-traditional industries experienced problems in finding clients. It would appear that the high knowledge and capital barriers to entry into non-traditional sectors account for this finding. Women starting businesses in non-traditional areas are unlikely to gain the considerable financial backing required unless they have developed an understanding of their potential markets and customer base. Achievement-orientated respondents constituted almost 65% of respondents in the new sectors. Few indicated that they had experienced problems in getting business. This supports the hypothesis that achievement-orientated women prepared well for business entry. The other respondents operating in new sectors were experiencing problems. The group most affected were the returners. In highly competitive markets women who organize their businesses around children, often working on a part-time basis, will find winning and retaining customers very difficult. This reflects the premium on customer care and technical support in these sectors.

There is a wide divergence between companies more or less than 5 years of age on the question of getting business and finding clients. Younger businesses experienced significantly fewer problems. Respondents identified three reasons for this. First, many experienced an initial surge of business gained by early enthusiastic marketing efforts. Second, clients were brought from previous employment. Despite this servicing these clients can leave little time for long-term market planning, particularly in service-based markets. Third, older businesses had consolidated their position in the marketplace and were looking at ways of financing expansion either of current market share or moving into new areas. This implied devoting management time to long term commercial development rather than selling to immediate customers.

Larger firms in the industry were seen to be more of a threat to respondent's business than competition from smaller firms (Tables 4.5 and 4.6). Of the 22 respondents who felt threatened by larger companies, 15 believed that large companies had an unfair advantage over smaller firms working within the same sector and locale. The issue goes beyond size of the company. It is shaped by clients' perceptions of the ability of the smaller company. Many respondents believed that gender was an aspect of this. A partner in a young architectural practice explained:

> Persuading people that we are a large enough firm to do larger projects is another problem, and I do think that I'm going to come up, more and more, against prejudice, because we are going to deal with larger firms which are run by men and who, I think, will feel less confident in our ability to undertake large projects.

Table 4.5 Is competition from firms in the area a problem?

	No.
From small firms	
Yes	15
No	45
Total	60
From larger firms	
Yes	22
No	38
Total	60

Table 4.6 If yes in Table 4.5, are larger firms perceived to have an unfair advantage?

	No.
Yes	15
No	7
Total	22

The strategy adopted by this particular respondent to overcome this problem was not one which all women could pursue. She continued:

> ... You're not going to get on with them anyway and there is plenty of work we can get from people who are more enlightened and who can accept us on the terms we are prepared to offer ourselves.

Some respondents were unequivocal in their belief that gender was a major factor in the problem of getting business (Table 4.7). The co-owner of a video engineering and training co-operative spoke in depth about the problem. She sold primarily to local authority and institutional buyers on a contract basis. She believed that discrimination on the basis of both gender and of the company structure was responsible for her inability to secure a place on tendering lists. Her strategy to overcome this was based on over-achievement and directly confronting negative attitudes:

> You have to get to the meeting early. You have to know what you want and also the minimum that you are prepared to accept. You have to be totally direct and, most of all, you must ensure that at no time do you lose face.

Conclusion

The business issues discussed in this chapter were considered by the respondents to be those which posed the greatest challenges to them as business owners. Although these problems can be seen as being common to all small business proprietors, they can also be interpreted as having a gender dimension. This was the case for a significant proportion of the women interviewed, many of whom believed that problem areas were exacerbated by their gender. While many business owners in the study perceived gender-related problems, others, with similar experiences, did not recognize problems as being gender related.

For many women, gender-related problems were directly attributable to two causes: their own self-confidence and their credibility as business owners. Two business owners summed up common feelings:

Table 4.7 Do you think that as a woman you are at a disadvantage in competing for orders or tending for contracts?

	No.
Yes	15
No	43
Don't know	2
Total	60

There is only one real difference between men and women which shows itself and that is confidence. A lot of men succeed because they think they can and that belief in oneself pushes you a long way forward. Also, I think that men are more used to feeling that they are in the business world—they see themselves in that kind of role.

I generally think that if a man gives the information, it's more likely to be considered accurate. Now, if a woman gives the information, it's more likely to be questioned or they think she doesn't know her stuff properly or something. I'm certain of that . . . If I were giving tips to people starting in business, be absolutely precise about what you want. Make sure you do everything professionally—it's very important for a woman.

For all of the respondents interviewed, the development of management strategies and a distinctive management style helped them to offset many of the problems. How the women developed management skills and the extent to which these helped in the day-to-day running of their businesses is discussed in the next chapter.

CASE STUDY

Company activity: *Publishers, Market Research Reports*
Company started: *May 1987*
Employees: *2*
Business organization: *Limited Company*

Company History

This respondent set up a company with two partners. The firm specializes in carrying out market research projects, and publishing and selling short reports. Subject areas tend to be specialized, concentrating on narrow product or market areas. Most reports are sold through carefully directed telephone campaigns.

The respondent gave up her job in publishing to have a baby in mid-1985 but was persuaded by a female ex-colleague, an accountant, to set up a small business providing word processing and desk-top publishing facilities to industry and commerce. After 1 year in business the respondent and her partner were approached by one of their clients to publish a series of market reports he had researched and written. After some discussion, the three joined together to form a new company, thereby bringing publishing, business and research skills together. The respondent and her original partner, however, still own the original company and this has been giving financial support and back-up to their new venture.

The respondent officially works part time, although when the business demands it she works at night and at the weekends when her husband is free to provide domestic and childcare support. To date, the respondent's priorities have still been with looking after her young son, although already there are signs that she is becoming more involved with the business. Self-employment had never been attractive to the respondent as her father, who inherited his father's paper and package wholesaling business, had found self-employment stressful and unrewarding. Since her original partner persuaded her to start up the first company, however, the respondent has grown to value the independence and control of her working environment offered through business ownership:

> Control over my own environment is very important. I didn't particularly want to do it and it wasn't that I wanted independence and control. I found myself sort of thrust into this. But, now I am in it, I find those things very valuable and that is why I would hate to give it up now. The independence and control of my own life.

Start Up

The three directors set up a limited company and financed it with loans amounting to £12 000. The company still operates from the basement of one of the director's houses. This has reduced overheads, freeing more capital for the purchase of publishing equipment.

Although the initial finance was completely made up of personal savings, the three directors produced a carefully produced business plan and cash flow projection, which they presented to their prospective bank manager. The respondent believes that, between the three directors, the company now has all the relevant skills for success.

One area in which the respondent is less confident is dealing with employees. Although she has had experience of supervising staff in previous employment, she feels that her position as owner/boss is more difficult to administer:

> Being a business owner has also made me aware of weaknesses in areas that I thought I was quite skilful. I am quite organized and that has come through quite well. I also thought I was quite good at dealing with people, on a sort of employer/employee level. I thought I was quite a good manager. Now I am not so sure. ... In one of my jobs I had a team of four people working for me. But, I also had a boss, and carrying out someone else's orders, when you know you have got their authority behind you is a lot easier.

Growth and Development

Although the business is still in its first year, it has already overgrown a number of aspects of the initial business plan. In addition, the respondent's earlier business has continued to grow, despite her concentration of effort in the newer company. By the time of the second interview the respondent was reassessing her approach to both businesses. The older business, which had been continued primarily to service the new venture, was becoming more successful, and was moving into new areas such as telephone marketing and telesales campaigns:

> Over the last three months our turnover on the market research side is exactly the same as the turnover on other jobs and we find ourselves wondering about our future direction. A lot of small companies quite often do this. They do other jobs to keep themselves afloat. So, we are still pushing ahead with our market research publishing, because, unlike the other jobs, this is something in which we have a lot of experience and skill, but it is also a business which takes a long time to establish.

In the long term the respondent and her fellow directors are likely to direct their energies towards the areas of business in which they have most confidence. Although the original financial plan has quickly become outdated, the respondent's financial director has continued to plan and assess the business' financial status and projected income. Earlier experience in producing pricing has been built upon, and pricing strategies developed:

> We have learned from our mistakes about pricing our services—not to price them too cheaply, for the sake of being competitive to cut your own throat. Because, now, the main thrust of our work is market research publishing, we decided we didn't really need other work. We have therefore priced ourselves on a sort of take it or leave it basis.

In terms of marketing strategies, the respondent and her fellow directors are in the process of developing plans for future expansion into Europe and other international markets, depending on their UK performance over the next 2 years.

The respondent's approach to her business has changed from an almost casual involvement to being much more active and committed. As the respondent developed support networks—made up of her husband, parents and neighbours—to provide care for her son, she was able to spend more time in the business. Her early doubts about self-employment were replaced by a recognition of its benefits. While her two fellow directors provide expertise and support, they also "share the burden of responsibility" once thought by the respondent to be a major disadvantage of business ownership. Finally, the current success and future growth potential of her company have also contributed to the change in the respondents attitude to her business:

> Now I see signs that perhaps the company could really grow, beyond perhaps even my expectations. That is quite exciting and the idea that I could have control over a smallish company, with a reasonable turnover, would be very satisfying. It is not something that motivated me in the beginning, but I can see it motivating me as the job progresses.

5

Female Entrepreneurs as Managers and Their Strategies for Success

The initial interviews provided some indication of how the women managed their businesses. The same interviews outlined the development of individual management styles. They gave some indication of their methods of coping with management problems, such as delegation and the establishment of systems. The follow-up interviews provided further insight into particular aspects of management including the development of management strategies to overcome barriers and the women's attitudes towards the management of growth.

Prior Experience

Previous working experience and training in management skills had a significant impact upon the development of management methods, skills and strategies for women business owners. Although only eight of the 60 respondents had been employed in management positions directly prior to self-employment, a further 12 had been engaged in technical or professional work. This proportion is higher than for the female population as a whole and reflects the relatively high career attainment of many of the respondents. Those who had previous management experience were predominantly within the achievement-orientated groups. They were able to adapt management skills, gained elsewhere, to self-employment:

> I was a manager, so obviously I have had management experience and management training. I've also been a trainer, so I've had training experience. So there was no problem in setting up a training programme. My degree is in organizational behaviour, so I have obviously had quite a lot of academic input, so my past career history has been quite useful.

> Managing my own business, I had a fair amount of ideas about. Having done the London Enterprise Agency small business course, and having been a manager and managed a budget. Also, I have been a sales person and lived on commission . . .

There was variation in respondents' attitudes to the value of pre-start-up management experience. Many women, particularly those in the returner and aspirant achiever groups, believe that the type of direct management experience needed in starting and running their businesses can be acquired once in business. A significant proportion of the entrepreneurs had experience of staff supervision, of sales and marketing and of general business administration. They could apply this to their business. Others gained their experience of management through domestic responsibilities. There was a widespread belief that skills developed as wives and mothers were just as valid as more formally acquired skills and could be applied to business management:

> I think when you have a family and a job, you have to be able to manage your life very carefully to balance the two. The actual management involved of just managing a home and a family is one form of management, quite a difficult form of management, and when you start bringing in outside interests and a career and a business you have to be a tremendous manager. I think any business woman and wife and mother has those skills or develops those skills. She has to, to be able to cope.

> I think that married women have an advantage over men in that they have been used to doing half a dozen things at once. Men often tend to be tunnel visioned, but a mother's experience teaches her to be different. She has to collect someone from the dentist at three o'clock; supervise the homework as well as understand it; cook a meal and then act as a taxi service. Women have the ability to think of half a dozen things at once and still keep the thing going.

There was no conclusive evidence on this. Some returners used their acquired skills to great effect. Others were less successful.

Conflicting Demands

Few achievement-orientated women supported the notion of combining full-time ownership of a growth-orientated business with bringing up children. For many achievement-orientated women, a determination to succeed required all their energy and could not include children. A pharmaceutical manufacturer stated:

You can't be serious about running a growing business and have to run and look after a child that's got measles. Basically, I think that if you want to have a business at that stage you must either have a nanny to look after them full time, or they must be in boarding school, mine were in boarding school, or you don't have children. You just completely and totally put yourself into your business. I think it's very difficult to be successful in both home and business and I do think it affects the children. Even my daughter says you're never here when I need you, although she's eighteen . . . I never for one moment felt that I would ever not succeed and went out with that attitude and I'm quite convinced that if you have got this formula that you have to be successful. Sure you need all the back up like your planning, your projections, your budgets, your plans, but they can all come initially if you see something and you know and you believe that and you are determined to make a success of it, you can. If you've got a basic knowledge of what to do, how to set it up, it all comes to you. But the two are not compatible.

This single mindedness was often a key management strategy.

Management Techniques

The range and nature of the management techniques employed by participants varied considerably. One described the management function as being concerned with "people, time and finance". Others found the concept of management difficult to define and rather alien. Some of the newer businesses operated informally but there was an acceptance that management functions would have to be formalized in the future. These businesses were so small they could be organized on an ad hoc basis, until growth was achieved:

> There have been a few problems but, generally, we just work it out for ourselves. You can get a text book to tell you what to do, but it doesn't always apply to small businesses . . . Because it's so small it's easy enough to handle but if it gets bigger it will be more difficult.

> I think it [management] is something you learn when one day you say, really, I have got to do something about this. For instance, we are really stuck for space here. I blame part of the bad management here on the lack of space. It is just impossible and it's the biggest problem, so now I'm doing something about it—moving to bigger premises.

Other respondents were keen to implement a distinctive management style as soon as their first employees were recruited. Their ability to undertake this successfully varied:

> I think I found the development of a management style a difficult thing, particularly because I first employed friends. It's that thing of inequality, of unequal relationships, that works both ways. Because you carry the can you

have responsibility. It tends to distort relationships you might have had previously. I think if I had a certain type of management experience it would have been a lot easier.

We tried to establish an open system of management which brings its own problems. But, we always tried to retain a sort of family feel, that we are well known by clients and staff and to retain that sort of spirit for the company. But it is more difficult with more people.

Value Driven

There was a widespread commitment to the notion of building 'value driven' businesses. These women stated that they were concerned that the atmosphere and general ethos of their company was open and flexible. This was reflected in the kind of management style which they wanted to adopt. For many, the emphasis upon open channels of communication, flexible systems, and the establishment of good interpersonal relationships, was cited as a major difference between male and female employers. A food manufacturer stated:

If you are working in a woman's world you have got to be flexible. You may not be in a big organization which has a creche, we're not that big and we can't afford to do that. But where we do need to accommodate we will. It is part and parcel of normal life, it is as simple as that. It is nice, you get a sense of how people are and how their children are, and it gives you a nicer feeling about them.

Although you have a lot of pressure, it is like happy families. I mean it is like running a business, there are so many pressures, but it is still a happy family. The models are under pressure as well because we have certain interruptions and things, alright, it's nice to have photographers, but they are interruptions when we don't need them and it holds us all back. But you're all under pressure at any fashion show and the thing is that if the show is successful then everybody is happy about it. There is a lot of satisfaction, even though it might be so hectic that you haven't time to think, it's very satisfying [model and promotions agency].

Not all respondents found their desired systems or management style easy to develop as the following examples illustrate. First, a Glasgow based data processing company:

It is difficult, I think, especially for me since I have not been used to dealing with what I call shop floor level. I had to modify my behaviour and change my sort of level of communication. So, I tend to talk more through my data prep manager. Although I keep in close contact with the girls, there are certain things I need translated for me.

Being a business owner has also made me quite aware of weaknesses in areas that I thought I was quite skilful. I am quite organized and that has come through quite well, I also thought that I was good at dealing with people on a sort of employer–employee level. I thought I was quite a good manager, now I'm not so sure ... In one of my jobs I had a team of four people working with me, but I also had a boss and was carrying out someone else's orders. When you know you have got their authority behind you it is a lot easier [aromatherapy mail order company).

Credibility

A young lingerie manufacturer found it difficult to establish herself as a credible employer until external confirmation of her ability was achieved:

Having to constantly assert myself—that is definitely changing. I think it is only because I'm becoming recognized through winning awards. That is the only way you can actually get that sort of credibility. There is no point saying, "well, I've been in business for 2 years, I know what you have to do so get on with it". The only way people perceive you is through your awards and things like that.

I'm not a hard person normally, but I'm having to be in some respects. I'm having to really put my foot down on some things. Unless I do, it just doesn't happen, so I find I'm having to be. But that is not me by nature. If I want to be successful I have to be. I should be even harder in a lot of cases [wine bar owner].

This approach to business relations suggests a marked difference between male and female business values. Women proprietors seem more anxious to develop group-based, consensus-driven ventures. This contrasts with the charismatic leader-based ventures of traditional entrepreneurs. The more ambitious and successful entrepreneurs saw the process of review and assessment as crucial to the management function. An essential feature of this, even for those without prior experience, was the ability to grasp opportunities and to take stock of current situations. This allowed their companies to grow in a distinctive, cohesive and controlled way. A business consultant explained how she used a lull in demand after the stock market crash to assess and subsequently renew her business:

Well, there are two ways it could have gone. It could have gone down the chute or we could have expanded and had a higher turnover. I saw that as the opportunity to get the business that we wanted and get the staff we wanted. The staff that were finding growth difficult had actually gone, and we were able to recruit people from university level. We now actually have people who can explore and develop and not get stuck in what they know.

For me it has always been really important to review continuously what is happening at the moment and what you want to happen, almost monthly. To review monthly exactly where you are and where you want to be going and how you want to get there, particularly in a new business, you need to continuously review the situation [health and leisure club owner].

This last year the focus of what I have been doing is gathering information and getting it to the point of where it is of some use where you can use it. I think information is power. If you do not know, at any one time, how much work you have got in hand, how long it is going to take you to do, and how much money you have got in the bank, and how much money is owed to you, then you don't know your business [industrial clothing manufacturer].

An almost compulsive desire to organize things was identified by certain respondents as a key personality feature. Respondents from all age groups and industrial sectors felt that organizational ability was an inherent part of their personalities.

Direct experience in management was a useful supplement to this but many respondents interpreted management skills as simple common sense.

Organizing is part of me I think. It's the same in my social life as well, I manage my friends. I'm not trying to be conceited or arrogant but it's true, I'm really good at saying well, what you need to do with your life is this . . . I'm like that with people all the time [ceramic designer].

Stress

Three management issues were especially stressful. These were the occasions when individual management styles and ability were tested. The issues which proved most taxing were usually connected with company growth and development. Typically, they occurred in the transitional period between formation of the new company and the development of an established, ongoing growth-orientated firm. Many respondents viewed the delegation of tasks, implementing systems and procedures and implementing strategic decision making (usually in connection with limiting the range and scope of the company) as the greatest sources of personal stress.

The ability to delegate effectively was closely linked with effective management styles and systems. It was a common problem for the respondents. Many women had learnt to delegate domestic and childcare commitments, but were still learning to delegate business-related tasks. Two major stages in the delegation process could be identified, first, the delegation of operational tasks such as book-keeping and accounting and second, the delegation of aspects of the management function itself.

These are the two post-entrepreneurial phases of the developing firm: professionalism and departmentalism.

The rate at which managers moved through these stages varied considerably. Some moved rapidly to the first stage, while for others, months or years passed before businesses reached this stage. These were traumatic times for two groups in particular: younger respondents and those with a strong need to retain control. Few of the former had any management experience, and they were concerned about the responsibility of becoming an employer.

> I'll always want to put my oar in, I suppose, especially on the designing side of it. And I certainly wouldn't like to get managerial, so that people couldn't come and talk to me. If I wasn't involved on the production side then I'd have to really trust the people I employed and I don't ever see myself being able to leave it all to someone else . . . I've got to keep control even if it means me working 24 hours a day, I prefer to know how things are going all the time. I'm always sacrificing my social life [textile designer and manufacturer].

> I find it difficult. Then if I do and something goes wrong, it is twice as difficult the next time to trust that the person has actually done it right. Having said that, I still think it can and should be done [secretarial services company].

> With the employee employer thing, I think I've got it better worked out now . . . I don't want to play it. I prefer not playing it but I know how to play it and I understand what it brings with it. It's not a solution but it's a reconcilement [textile finishing company].

For some younger, achievement-orientated women, the need to delegate was brought about by a conflicting pressure of needing to reduce the hours spent in the business. As Table 5.1 demonstrates, just under half of

Table 5.1 Hours worked per week.

Hours	No. of respondents
0–10	0
11–20	3
21–30	4
31–40	12
41–50	13
51–60	14
61–70	9
71–80	3
81–90	1
91–100	1

the respondents worked in excess of 50 hours a week, with some working as many as 80–100 hours. A significant majority (72%) stated that they worked longer hours than they did prior to starting in business.

> I think there is a culture that would say that hard work means success and that you don't get to work only 35 hours a week and be successful as well. My great conversion has been that now I believe that I can work 35 hours a week and have a successful big company as well . . . It is a sort of discipline if you like, to keep myself in check to maintain a balance and not to go bananas. At least I do it out of enthusiasm now, rather than , "Oh, I've got to do this". When I was working long hours before I was working on production. Producing rather than managing [lingerie manufacturer].

> I think if you are working 20 hours a day you are not working well and you are not working efficiently. If I am doing that I know I'm making a lot of mistakes. The guy I live with now, he really leant on me hard about the number of hours I was working and the time he was getting out of me. I am actually very glad that he does that, I think it is very good for me because it doesn't stop the company growing at all. The number of hours you put in is not about making the company grow [social photographer].

For women who had a strong need to control, the underlying causes of their difficulty in delegating were related to their previous experience in employment and their motivations for choosing self-employment. A number of respondents moved into self-employment in response to perceived discrimination in terms of promotion and recognition while working for large companies. Self-employment was seen as a means of gaining control over their work and status, or tackling subordination. Consequently, delegation was a difficult skill to acquire. For a few respondents this translated into suspicion about professional business advisers:

> Interest payments could have crippled us and also control by the banks. I'm very much against involving the banks. The banks have a great control and you really cannot implement your own strategy, you are continually reporting to them. And their objectives are different, they want their money back whereas we take a longer term view of it.

Delegation

Respondents recognized the importance of delegating tasks if their businesses were to grow and they acknowledged their difficulties with this.

> The thing is you just have to delegate, because it's no good trying to be a superman or a superwoman. You've got to delegate and I think the basic is to have a good staff and it's taken me 3 years to get into a position where I can go away quite happily for a week or a fortnight. I planned it that way [advertising agency].

A lot of women suffer from the superwoman complex, thinking that they will do as well in business as they can, all by themselves. It is a philosophical attitude. I think I have to become less of a perfectionist. Taking my family and the person that I work with and her family into account, and the weather, and all the variables that there are in my line of work [garden maintenance partnership].

Recognition of the need to delegate at an early stage was closely associated with management success. A number of businesses had reached the stage where a further degree of delegation was necessary. This was when management and decision making had to be shared. This usually occurred when the business had developed to the extent that an additional manager was needed. Those who had successfully tackled this stage emphasized the value of good communications networks, and keeping employees involved in decisions.

The largest employer in the sample described the decision-making processes in her company:

A perfect example is a very large change in organization which we have been working on for some months. When everything was ready we brought the managers in and we had a meeting and asked if there were questions, if anyone had any worries, or had a different point of view, they could have said and then it would have been up to management. The management made the decision and if any senior manager had not been happy then we would have had a re-think. Once the senior management had been told then it was up to us to bring everybody in and say what was going on, and up to us to show the benefits and tell them what was going on [financial services company].

The approach adopted was typical of the traditional family firm. Senior managers from outside the family were not involved until the three family directors had made the initial decision. This respondent left the day-to-day running of her business to her managers but reserved certain issues for the family. Few respondents involved staff in major decisions. Many seemed willing to give up a degree of control but acknowledged their fears in this issue.

Well, I will have to delegate. I may lose control, direct control, of the small, everyday things but I'm quite happy to do that. I would not ever see myself losing control of the business.

The development of more sophisticated systems and procedures, beyond the *ad hoc* decision making usually utilized at start up, became more important as companies became more established. The owners of a private language school illustrated their need:

We have only just realized it now, but it was a question of one person doing it all and the business had grown out of that. Marion was away for a week and the whole system just collapsed, nobody could put their hands on things. Nobody knew which host families had been paid and which hadn't. So this was really the problem. It hit us very hard, especially as at the time we were busy coping with the summer school—it's a 24 hour job—and although we realized the inaccuracy of the system, there was just no way we could step outside of it.

A manufacturer of swimming pools reiterated the need for effective systems, preferably at the start-up stage:

It sounds very simple when you are starting up and you can't type—you get a typist. But it becomes a lot more complicated as the business develops . . . Starting up systems and priorities, I can't stress how important they are 7 years hence. I'm thinking of my own situation in business. They are as applicable today and more difficult to recognize because you are so used to sailing through and making decisions. It's hard to stop and say "look, I'm getting myself into a muddle".

As businesses grew in terms of owner experience, employment size and turnover, respondents began to realize the need for a more strategic approach to decision making. Some businesses in this sample had reached this stage, but for those that had the realization came after a period of crisis which had forced a radical restructuring in the way that the business operated.

An electronic typesetting and publishing company had faced either company closure or a restructuring:

We have learned from our mistakes about pricing our services, not to price them too cheaply for the sake of being competitive to cut your own throat. Because, now, the main thrust of our work is market research publishing, we decided we didn't really need any other work. We have therefore priced ourselves on a sort of take it or leave it basis . . . So, we're on the brink. We could close or we could expand and have a higher turnover. I see this as an opportunity to get the business that we want. The thing is, the customers that aren't coming back are the ones we can do without. They bring in some money, sure, but not anything that would make the bank manager happy. So, we now have to have the faith, if you like, to go for the customers that make the bank manager happy, which means chasing a bit more in the city or chasing bigger publications or straightforward things.

A freelance film producer had also decided to limit the range and scope of her business to the contracts that were most profitable:

You take on every job that comes through the door, which means that some jobs are less profitable than others. You can become an overall jack of all trades, but a master of none. You find that you are doing all sorts of odds and sods. Now, I had to do that when I first started out and I grew along these lines until I could not cope because I didn't have (a) the experience and (b) I didn't know how to employ people . . . However, now I know the type of work I want and I can afford to be more selective . . . so that I will do fewer, more profitable jobs, but each of these jobs is worth more and more profit.

Management Strategies

The development of formalized management strategies is closely linked to the management styles developed by individual respondents. Strategies are often developed to cope with and counteract gender-related difficulties. Goffee and Scase (1985) interpret business ownership, in itself, as being a strategy to overcome labour market-related gender subordination. In this study, the data suggest that women confront gender-related problems within proprietorship. Consequently, they need to develop strategies to overcome these. A number of women recognized that they had deliberately adopted certain strategies. Others evolved strategies or developed approaches incrementally as their firms grew. During this time their management styles also become more sophisticated.

Strategies to combat a generally perceived lack of credibility, to gain confidence, and to prove capability were dominant. Three common approaches were used: investment in training in business and management skills; an increased interest in 'professionalizing' themselves and their businesses; and the use of networking. These strategies were by no means mutually exclusive, but were part of a portfolio of approaches adopted to suit certain situations at different times. The more successful women in the study showed considerable style flexibility. They avoided being locked into a single conventional style. The dominant management styles tended to be high in both relationship orientation and achievement orientation.

Training as a Management Strategy

The view that it is the lack of prior experience which differentiates women and men in business was common among the respondents. For young women, without the benefit of either prior management or often work experience, this situation was exacerbated. Many reacted by consciously developing a management strategy which enabled them to compensate for youth as well as gender. This generally consisted of rigorous planning prior to start-up, attendance at business training programmes and intensive and extensive use of the available external resources and advisory agencies.

Formal training in business was only part of this. The more successful respondents were very aware of the benefits of learning business and management skills by watching others. This enabled them to build up their own confidence while reinforcing consciously developed and individual styles of dealing with people.

> I think, through the courses I did, I got to acknowledge how far I'd come and what I was actually doing, instead of wondering if I was doing it right. You can evaluate whether you are in line with your goals or not through the results that you can get. It enables you to grow more and to expand personally [publisher].

> The courses were very important for me because I lacked so much information. It was difficult, particularly learning about myself. You had to analyse yourself, it was horrendous at the time but worth it in the end [soft furnishings manufacturer].

> I have had to develop many more selling skills and had to learn to be able to chat on the telephone and do things like that, where before I was purely creative. I now have to go beyond that in order to sell that creativity, because business is much more than writing [freelance copy writer].

> I now find that people find me intimidating and I find that difficult to believe, but there is one guy here who is in his late fifties who just finds me incredibly intimidating which I think is just extraordinary. So, I must have that authority now. It is actually something that I am aware of—I have watched how one of my partners deals with people and he is actually very rude—but I have watched how he does it, it is all an attitude of mind. I feel now quite differently from when I first started [advertising agency].

The deliberate and systematic search for knowledge, credibility and self-confidence was a recurrent theme in respondents' strategies for success. Many of the respondents displayed a willingness to watch and learn from others and an acceptance of their own weaknesses.

Professionalization as a Management Strategy

Another strand in the development of personal strategies to cope with managing a business was to become more professional and adopt the norms set by other business professionals. This strategy was used by many respondents to overcome gender-related problems. These, generally older, women sublimated their gender and personal position to gain credibility and confidence in the eyes of others. This approach was strongly associated with market success especially in the early period of business development. Evidence of the success of this strategy was apparent in a number of situations and was commonly used to disguise any potential gender issue. One woman spoke of how she had to take "the whole issue of my sex out of the way".

The two frequently identified situations in which this approach was used were raising finance and competing for orders. Detailed prior preparation was a powerful theme. Besides preparing well for interviews with potential lenders, they sent business plans in advance and researched the area thoroughly. They took this further by determined efforts at role playing. They wore business suits to create an aura of efficiency and competence and to put the bank managers at ease. Women spoke of using initials rather than full forenames on stationery. They consciously chose to use male business partners or members of staff to represent the company when dealing with clients. Those who adopted a strategy of professionalization were confident of their own ability but doubted the ability of others to recognize it.

> Although it's usually me who deals with the technical work, when we're negotiating a contract or tender my partner deals with them... I do think that I am going to come up more and more against prejudice from men who, I think, will feel less confident about my ability [video engineering and training company].

> I don't often come up against problems, even though I'm a woman in a rather unusual environment. Although I'm doing a big job on a building site at the moment and they'll tend to come up and say "I haven't seen a woman here before" or "why aren't you at home". You have to have the right answer at the right time [industrial photographer].

This 'sublimation' of their femininity was a deliberately chosen and very successful strategy. In contrast, some women entrepreneurs believed that their gender gave them certain advantages and improved their situation in certain areas of business ownership. This view was not restricted to women working in traditionally female sectors.

> Actually, builders anywhere respond much better to a woman. If you tell them to do something they feel they can't swear at you and they don't know how to deal with that. So in that respect I found no problems at all [architecture practice].

> One thing very noticeable when you go to a lot of business conferences, meetings, enterprise shows, Chamber of Commerce—you are in a minority.

The last Chamber of Commerce dinner we were at, there were four or five women out of 200 people. That has its advantages. People remember you because you are a woman. If you talk to them "Oh, yes. You were at such and such" [swimming pool builder].

Others did not believe that professionalization was necessary or even compatible with female management styles:

It is probably a generalization to say this but I have more trouble in managing and dealing with women, or rather 'honorary men'. It is the pin stripe suit ladies that I particularly do not get on with because I don't think it is a style that is necessary. I think that women have a lot of innate qualities that are better for management than trying to be dressed as a man [market research consultancy].

Gender was commonly used as an effective aid to business development.

Networking as a Management Strategy

A common strategy used by respondents at different stages of business ownership was the development of a network of people able to advance their ambitions of proprietorship. For many women, networking had formed a major part of the pre-start strategy to gain advice and information as well as provide informal market research. Some women had used networking as a strategy to enable them to move from part-time to full-time trading. In one instance, a hairdresser working freelance in evenings and weekends was able to develop a network of clients to ensure enough full-time customers to enable her to become self-employed.

More experienced women and women working in predominantly male sectors used networking as a means of establishing themselves in an industry or sector.

... I had worked for a large company, I am very used to being at conferences and so on and my reputation had spread. So McDonald Douglas, from whom I now license my equipment paid me a personal visit, and have now gained confidence in me [light engineering manufacturer].

Each year we have a project, last year the project was a new brochure for the company. A couple of years ago, maybe about 5 years into the business, I felt that I needed to break into the establishment. Because I am a woman, and because I work in isolation in a specialized industry, I wanted to meet and try to contact and be involved socially with my peers within the industry, architects, quantity surveyors etc., so I made a conscious effort to go out and join things like the Institute of Directors [swimming pool builder].

You cannot draw on old boys networks until you have established yourself as having credibility. Being able to be relied upon . . . I think you've got to develop your credibility first and then consolidate your contacts [textile manufacturer].

Those women who were more confident of their success, joined professional associations for enjoyment rather than for gain.

A Glasgow-based engineer who has witnessed the decline of British manufacturers specializing in her product in favour of cheaper imported components now owns the only existing plant of its kind in Scotland. Her company has increased its market share and profitability ratio every year since she bought it.

Not only am I the only female member of my professional trade association, I am the first woman member since it started in the eighteenth century. I go to all their dinners, the only woman and the only smoker, they really hate it!

Other women used business networks as a method of gaining independent and objective assessments of business performance.

I have often thought about having a sort of supervisor, like when you are at university—a tutor or something. That would be really good, someone who perhaps saw you every 2 months in a group of five or six people. They really wouldn't necessarily need particular skills apart from a general knowledge of business, just a good listener almost. So you could talk out your problems and where you were and what you thought about it. Because its actually quite isolated, running a small business. The more opportunities you get to talk to people who aren't directly involved who can often see things you can't see, the better.

Networking was a response to the isolation of business ownership. Several women were involved in semi-formal business clubs, often arising from business training courses. In this respect, training for business ownership can also be seen as an initial stage in the development of business networks, particularly for young women unlikely to have sufficient contacts before they start up.

Some respondents identified a need for women-only networks. Others were ambivalent about formalized single sex organizations, but acknowledged that they used female business friends as informal contacts for advice. Many of the achievement-orientated women with established businesses were aware that they could be seen by younger women as potential role models. They were generally keen to develop networks as a strategy to help other women in business.

Networking can be seen as the most commonly used and most generally effective of all strategies employed by women in business. All respondents used business and informal networks at one or more stage of business development. Frequently it was a permanent strategy used at all times and often in conjunction with other strategies to overcome the problems, usually gender related, of proprietorship.

Once they had undertaken the first stages of transition from new companies to established firms, many respondents had developed ideas of how they envisaged further company growth. Some women, although orientated towards growth in the long term, were trying to limit expansion until they were certain that they could control the growth and when it would be more suitable to them personally. The issue of how different groups of women approached growth is examined in greater depth in Chapter 6.

In conclusion, it can be seen that there is some variation in the management challenges that women entrepreneurs face. The previous experience of management and business ownership has an effect on how well women cope with these challenges. The range and sophistication of management techniques at their disposal also varied. In terms of management strategies, however, clear patterns emerge among women entrepreneurs. Training, professionalization and networking were the favoured and most accessible of all strategies at their disposal.

CASE STUDY

Company activity:	*Design and Construction of Swimming Pools*
Company started:	*1980*
Employees:	*12*
Business organization:	*Sole Trader*

Company History

Throughout her life this respondent has been in close contact with small businesses, principally a small coal mine in Lanarkshire. Her mother owned a hotel and catering business and her husband is also self-employed.

After leaving school and during the early years of the respondent's married life, she worked on a casual basis for her father's businesses. As she had not achieved any formal qualifications at school, the respondent used her years of part-time working to participate in a wide variety of Open University business and engineering courses. As her children grew older, the respondent became involved in a partnership in a small agricultural equipment sales and construction company, on a part-time basis. However, in 1979, the partnership was dissolved as the business ran into trouble. The respondent felt that as a woman working in part-time capacity, she was unable to influence major decisions made by her partners.

The respondent set up her company in 1980. Since then, her company has gained a reputation throughout Scotland as a small but growing supplier of luxury swimming pools. The company now employs 12 people and contracts in numerous others when necessary. The company is profitable, with profits making up 22% of net turnover, and 40% of gross.

As the respondent has become active in a number of employers' and small business organizations, she herself has also become relatively well known in local business circles, both within and outside her own industry.

Start Up

After leaving her original company, the respondent lacked confidence about her skills in the business, and more significantly, the likelihood of gaining finance for future ventures. With the encouragement of her husband and a number of potential clients, however, the respondent looked at ways of utilizing skills and contracts gained in her previous business. Through her involvement in the construction side of her earlier company, she had become aware of the potential of swimming pool design and construction. She therefore set about planning and financing her new enterprise.

As a mother of two young children, the respondent had been working on a part-time basis until starting the new company. Although she admits to feeling 'guilt pangs' about leaving her children, often to work 80 hours a week in the first years, she believes her friend was accurate when she said, "You may be a terrible mother, working all hours, but you would be just as awful if you didn't."

As her previous company had not been financially successful, the respondent believed that she would not be considered for a bank loan or credit facility. Any new company would have to be self-financing. For the first time in her working career, she took a job, working for the Manpower Services Commission as a part-time co-ordinator on the Government's Springboard Scheme. She used all of her annual salary of £6000 to finance the swimming pool venture, but, surprisingly, this business was able to survive and grow using only that source of initial finance.

Overheads were kept to a minimum in a number of areas. The respondent used her home as a base. As her house is large enough to allow adequate space for the administrative side of her business and is also used to display one of the respondent's swimming pool designs, this location has worked well for the business. At the time of writing the respondent could rely on contacts made previously to supply her first contracts and so limit advertising costs. Labour costs were also controlled. As is typical in the construction industry, workers were contracted in to carry out specific jobs, and, while the business was small, the respondent was able to administer much of the business herself. One business practice, established by the respondent early on, involves the prompt payment of bills. Perhaps as a consequence of her early lack of confidence in asking for credit for her business, the respondent always pays her bills on time, and expects similar treatment from her customers. In this she seldom has problems, as most of her work is contract based and paid in stages. Should payment not be forthcoming, the work would not continue.

Growth and Development

Using her long experience in small business, the respondent established a series of practices which still influence her style of management. An important ability for the small business owner, according to the respondent, is to be able to recognize weaknesses and buy in the appropriate skills:

> You should be expounding all your energy into what you're good at. You should be able to earn enough money to pay somebody else to do it better than you can do it, and you should recognize it. Whether it's baking scones, washing socks or typing letters. You should recognize that.

In terms of planning for growth, the respondent has developed a series of annual projects, either for herself, or for her business:

> Each year, we have project. Last year the project was a new brochure for the company. We hadn't had one before and it was quite a high expenditure. Also, very time consuming. A couple of years before that, I felt—maybe about 5 years into the business—I felt that I needed to break into establishment. Because I'm a woman, because I work in a specialist industry. I wanted to meet and try and involve socially or contact socially, my peers, within the industry.

As the respondent is the only female owner of a swimming pool construction business in her area, and as women are very much in the minority in the industry as a whole, the respondent has actively sought out a formal network of business friends. She has also joined a variety of management and small business organizations, including the Institute of Directors and British Institute of Management. Apart from offering her business support, the respondent has identified these organizations as being a potential source of custom.

In recent years, as her company has grown, the respondent has become increasingly aware of her own managerial limitations, and is currently exploring ways of delegating those functions for which she does not feel qualified:

> It sounds very simple when you're starting up and you can't type. You get a typist. But it becomes a lot more complicated as the business develops . . . Starting up procedures and priorities, I can't stress how important they are

7 years hence. I'm thinking of my own situation in business. They are equally as applicable today and more difficult to recognize because you are so used to sailing through and making decisions. But it's hard to stop and say, "look, I'm getting myself in a muddle here".

During the next 2 years, the respondent has already formulated 'projects' or objectives for her business. This year she hopes to "see a consolidation of business principles". Next year, the respondent intends to look at new markets, and areas in which she is particularly interested. In the longer term, the respondent is in the process of developing strategies for her business. During the next few years, the respondent intends to concentrate on the technical side of her business, while delegating many of the management functions to an assistant, as yet not recruited. Now in her early fifties, the respondent hopes to either have sold her business in 10 years time, or to be taking an executive role.

The respondent has clearly developed views of advice and training needs of small, but established and growing businesses. One major gap in training provision, the respondent suggested, was in the areas of training, on day release or short block basis, of small business staff:

I would love my secretary to go out and have day courses, or week long courses in other environments but it is just impossible to find. I mean it is not necessary for her personally but generally, for middle management in small companies. That is totally different to middle management in big companies. There is a great deal of isolation at all levels.

In terms of advice, the respondent suggested that there is a lack of specialist advice available to small businesses. Although she believes there is an adequate amount of general advice and information available, in later stages small businesses develop needs in particular areas. At present, in her view, these are not being met by business advice agencies.

Under the guidance of the respondent, this business is growing rapidly. However, the major decisions which will arise during the next few years are likely to concern the respondent's own personal needs. Having established and consolidated her business the respondent is in the process of deciding what role she wishes to play in her company's future.

6

The Dynamics of Enterprise and How Female Entrepreneurs Measure Success

Five distinct groups of respondents emerged from an analysis of their common motivations and experiences. These were *accidentalists*, young women who had drifted into self-employment; *aspirants*, young achievement-orientated women who viewed proprietorship as a long-term career option; *proven achievers*, older, achievement-orientated women who moved into business ownership to satisfy career ambitions; *re-entrants*, women returning to economic activity; and *traditionalists*, women who have inherited, through their families, a tradition of self-employment. This classification is an analytical tool to identify similarities and patterns of behaviour. In this respect, it resembles Weber's 'ideal types'. They were, however, behaviourial classifications which focused upon motivations at the pre-start and start-up stages of entrepreneurship and not categories which respondents necessarily belonged to for any extended period of time. They describe a pattern of behaviour at a stage in development.

Personal and career-related experience and attitudes towards business ownership form the initial basis for group classification. These also had an impact on the type of firm started. They determined the style of management used by the entrepreneur. The achievement-orientated groups, aspirants and proven achievers tended towards non-traditionally female sectors such as construction, engineering and manufacturing, as well as constituting the majority of proprietors within the new sectors business services and new technology-based industries. The remaining three groups, re-entrants, accidentalists and traditionalists, were disproportionately represented in traditionally female sectors (retail, service, hotel and catering). The accidentalists were characterized by their choice of sectors where barriers to entry were perceived to be low. A lack of education and training in specialist fields barred non-qualified re-entrants and traditionalists from starting businesses in more technically

98

demanding fields. The extent to which personal, and these were largely domestic, commitments could be accommodated also affected the choice of industrial sector.

Although the group classification was not dependent upon analysis of management style, differences did emerge between the groups. More noticeable, however, was the influence of age and experience upon styles of management. A maternalistic style, characterized by a unitaristic view of employee relations, was frequently adopted by older women within the high achiever and re-entrant groups. In contrast, younger women were drawn towards a more democratic style. Management experience did not directly affect company growth; this was determined largely by initial motivations for and different attitudes towards proprietorship at any given point.

The Dynamics of Enterprise

The type of change which occurred within the firms could not be accounted for by traditional static views of female entrepreneurial behaviour as defined by earlier studies (cf. Watkins and Watkins, 1984; Goffee and Scase, 1985). Qualitative data emphasized the dynamic and fluid nature inherent in female entrepreneurship. Initial motivations for start-up emphasized the need to fulfil personal objectives. Changes in personal goals have a direct impact upon the nature and objectives of the ongoing firm. Personal goal change which could impact upon the business was brought about by two factors. First, shifts in the respondents' personal (domestic) circumstances. These were most frequently due to the decision to have children. Second, there was direct experience of business ownership.

Specific women moved from one category to another. This was usually on the basis of business experience and personal attitude. As such, the groups reflect and highlight the fluid and dynamic nature of the sample. Movement from one category to another was not, however, universal. Traditionalists were unlikely to fundamentally change either their businesses or in their attitude towards business ownership. In other situations the pattern of movement was predetermined (*viz.* proven achievers could not convert to aspirants). Elsewhere, the patterns were fluid with internal and external factors capable of triggering change.

Accidentalists

Women who had drifted into business were the most likely to move from their initial mode of entrepreneurship. Respondents in the accidentalist group had been pushed into self-employment as an alternative to unemployment. They start with only a minimal interest in the direction and future of the company. Change was common among these women. This was frequently precipitated by pressure from external sources, such as parents, to sustain the enterprise. Typically, it reflected a new attitude towards entrepreneurship brought about by direct experience of business ownership. Change therefore could have one of two effects. Accidentalists could, after a positive experience of business ownership, become highly motivated and committed business owners, and progress to aspirants. Negative experience of business ownership could have the opposite effect of pushing them out of business.

Aspirants

For the aspirants, entrepreneurship was seen as an alternative long-term career option. Some move into proprietorship from full time education, their only experience of employment being temporary vacation jobs. Aspirants compensated for their lack of business and management experience by undertaking rigorous training courses and developing useful social and business networks. Their youth and lack of relevant business and career-related experience differentiated them from the group of proven achievers, many of whom had come out of 'high flying' careers. Having established themselves as business owners, aspirants could, however, progress to this grouping.

Proven Achievers

Proven achievers showed the same strong achievement orientation. They were older, with extensive career-related experience. Many already had children and did not predict further changes in their personal lives that would significantly affect their involvement in the business. This group was the most likely to be continuously growth orientated. Many of this group use proprietorship as a means to gain the flexibility to have both a family and a career. Some decided to have children and consequently reduce their personal involvement in the company. This had different effects. These depended upon the sophistication of the firm's management structure. For some, business became a part-time career as women spent time with their children. They converted their entrepreneurial mode to resemble re-entrants. Others developed their firms to the point that when they chose to have children, businesses were continued by partners and senior management.

This flexibility is not seen in other fields of entrepreneurial activity. In part, it reflects a lack of control over the relationship between family and business. A male business owner would not be forced to make these choices. In another sense it illustrates the liberating influence of business ownership. The woman can control the relationship between her work and her family.

Re-entrants

Women returning to economic activity had quite different experiences. They often came from management and career backgrounds. Re-entrants had already taken career breaks to have families. Businesses were specifically planned and started on a part-time basis to accommodate young families and involvement remained minimal. This sometimes persisted for several years. Business ownership was seen as a long-term career and income investment. When re-entrants progressed into full-time ownership they intended their businesses to grow accordingly. Growth indicated a move into a mode of proprietorship characterized by proven achievers. This group share many similar characteristics with the 'domestics' cited by Goffee and Scase (1985). They differ on one important point. Re-entrants, in this study, were highly aware of gender-related barriers present in the formal labour market. They were often the most radical in their feminist beliefs. This, in most cases, can be seen as a function of their previous experience as high flyers frustrated by gender-related career blocks.

Traditionalists

Traditionalists did not generally display the intergroup movement and dynamism of the other groups, although there were examples of women who changed their entrepreneurial mode. This largely reflected changes in personal situations, such as motherhood, as opposed to change through direct experience of business ownership. In these cases, attitudes towards business ownership appeared to replicate those of re-entrants, with a (temporary) emphasis upon family commitments rather than business growth. In the few instances in which this occurred the women often had a network of family members able to assume temporary responsibility for the business.

The Business Development Cycle

For this particular sample, the business development cycle is best explained in terms of incremental growth from the pre-start stages through entrepreneurial management, professionalization and finally managerial functionalism. Despite the relative newness of many of the firms, most had developed beyond the pre-start stages into entrepreneurial management. A minority had made the transition from entrepreneurial management to the stage which required the professionalization of the firm. Only two firms progressed to the point where their ventures stabilized and were managed at a functional level.

The move into entrepreneurial management from the pre-start situation poses a wide range of managerial and personal challenges to any individual starting in business. It normally involves extensive but calculated risk, with a number of barriers to entry being faced by prospective owner-managers. For women, the problems may be greater and, due to their general lack of prior experience, the risks higher. The distinction between periods of transition and other times is especially important. Transition is likely to be associated with: turbulence; increased risk and the non-formal management skills such as networking and flexibility with 'achievement orientation and motivation' important determinants of success or failure (Cannon, 1987). The ensuing periods; professionalism and functionalism, demand planning and the effective use of more formal management tools.

For the five groups of women identified in this study, the desirability of immediate growth beyond the stage of entrepreneurial management varied. Aspirants and proven achievers invariably saw growth as the logical progression of the company, but even so, wanted to control the rate of expansion.

> Now, I'm in the situation where I have got to make changes. Change is always quite difficult and I'm having to make changes after 6 months of very hard work and I'm tired. I would say that this is the first difficult situation I have had to overcome. Because I feel tired, I feel less motivated. Because I feel less motivated the changes I have got to make seem bigger than in fact they are [antiques restorer].

> The short-term objective has been to get the new gym opened and then we will revise what we are doing, whether we franchise the chain, or whether

we sell up or whether we start something different. I personally do not want to have a chain of health clubs that I'm responsible for, because I know what a responsibility it is [health and leisure club owner].

We have got a framework for development and growth. Although it seems that we grew out of that framework much more quickly than we had anticipated and we are growing very much along the lines that we designed. But it is difficult to know when to stop and where and when it is going to stop and whether we will get to a point when we don't want to get any larger. When we reach the ideal size I suppose—full productivity, profitability and happiness [graphic designer].

Management of growth was achieved by the use of techniques such as networking and flexibility. These are used in conjunction with more formal techniques which were learnt through previous management experience or by training for business ownership.

One aspirant had started as a designer of lingerie before moving into manufacturing. She described how she had grown her company beyond the entrepreneurial management stage:

I wasn't Janet Reager and in the fashion industry there is so much snobbery in having a name and a label. It is so important in my price bracket. It was very hard to get retailers to actually buy from us. A big hurdle . . . we did a lot of promoting through fashion shows, getting a lot of press coverage, which was really then aiming at the consumer who would then go to the retailer and say, "have you got any . . .?", and that way we actually overcame that. You know, chapping on doors, going round and round again. We just couldn't get any one to buy in the beginning. But it was then going to the consumer, making them aware of who we were and then going into shops and asking them. Then we managed to get orders coming in.

This respondent, like other achievement-orientated women, re-searched the market and examined other businesses to learn of the common pitfalls. The appreciation that successful businesses stay 'close to the customer' and are unafraid to investigate other's mistakes, was apparent in many of the growth-orientated firms in the sample. While growth and diversification were carefully planned for, there was a common appreciation for the necessity of flexibility. The respondent continued:

I am trying to keep a ceiling on the rate of expansion of my business. I think it's quite easy to expand very quickly and end up in an overtrading position. I'm now aware of that because we are putting restriction upon export deals. We will only produce so many garments—it's a limited edition. Because I am aware that that's what happens in an industry like my own, we have put limited editions on the market so we know what we can produce. . . . You have to be prepared to look at other things. We took baby clothes on over the summer when we were quite quiet and we are also diversifying into cushions and things like that for Christmas.

For many women, the sector in which they traded dictated how growth was to be achieved. For some women, growth could only be maintained by employing more people, in particular, bringing in a new tier of middle management.

It would alleviate a lot of my problems because at the moment I'm trying to do literally everything and I feel that the time has come where there has got to be some weight taken off me. So if I had what you call two area managers they could negotiate with the supervisors and cut down on some of my attendance at meetings and training sessions. They can do some more ongoing training and they can be over the country as well as myself and it helps to build up a more efficient structure. I will have a structure, I'll have myself, my secretary and area managers who will do the training as well, supervisors and then the merchandisers [merchandising company].

You can push your distributors so far and unless you keep at them all the time they don't respond too well. Even in the UK where we have seen our one product go really well, we still have to keep on at them to push the new products. This is an area where we can actually expand quite dramatically by taking on our own sales team [pharmaceutical manufacturer].

One entrepreneur who had deliberately employed women as part of her management style experienced problems when she wanted to expand employment in the company. Her initial wish was to promote internally:

I have a very good team of girls, some have worked for us ever since we started, either part time, full time or whatever, who can manage accounts and certainly do the data base, but cannot really go in at the board and most of them don't want to because most are married with children and like working part time. So we have built ourselves up a hierarchy with people who actually don't want to be promoted [advertising agency].

Other achievement-orientated women achieved growth through diversification into new markets or through the introduction of new technology. The owner of a Nottingham-based merchandising company explained how her company had to constantly innovate to retain its market lead:

We are very up to date. We were the first company to launch these little hooked hangers which are necessary for the new style of garment presentation in shops. Everything is on rails now, so we were very up to date with that. We got one step ahead, and you've got to present developments pretty early because it takes a couple of years for it to filter through to the chain stores. We have another new development which we hope to launch early next year. . . . Last year we needed something and it wasn't available so we built it ourselves. We are the first company to ultrasonically weld plastics. I have got a very good director in the factory who is a brilliant craftsman and between us I get the ideas and he has to do the work. But it works very well.

For women who had drifted into business, the shift from pre-start to entrepreneurial management determined those which would remain viable.

Positive experiences of business ownership would invariably lead accidentalists to aspirant or achiever status where growth would be managed accordingly. For this group, development had to be made to another mode of entrepreneur before growth was successful. Management skills had to be acquired for profitable company development.

Re-entrants deliberately curtailed growth until other, domestic factors had been satisfied. The ability to sustain enthusiasm and impetus for future development during non-growth phases and the management of a non-growth company were especially demanding. A former ceramic designer, now working in the area of management consultant, explained:

> I wouldn't have liked to have that conflict when the children were smaller, it was important that they came first. So I kept the level of that pottery business to suit me. I didn't want anything else . . . whereas now I can expand a bit, but you know it does have its problems.

The traditionalists' experience of business ownership and their motivations for starting in business mitigated against future development. Few desired growth beyond either the entrepreneurial management or at the very most professionalization stages. Movement to the first and second stages of the business development cycle were effected by networking and the ability to draw on family experience and support. Few, however, saw business ownership in terms of sustained growth and development; the majority desired small-scale businesses to satisfy personal goals. The owner of a design consultancy which has grown beyond the intended size explained that she now wished to pursue different business interests:

> For a very long time the company was very precious to me. It was part of starting the company up, and having been very independent for a long time, it makes it difficult to think of being employed by someone else. Also, for a very long time I thought that the company was my life's work, but I don't know if that is so anymore. It could be that being taken over or going to the stock market would allow me to do something else. . . . For me it is

personal, it is all independence over my own life within the structure that I have created. .... For that reason I have come to the conclusion that I am probably better in start-up situations than I am in big company situations. That sounds contrary, but you have got a lot more control over a small set up than you have over a large one.

The need for female owner-managers to use strategies, such as networking, to offset gender-based barriers has been discussed in Chapter 5. It is likely that the willingness to use such strategies may allow female owner-managers to develop non-formal management skills to help them through periods of transition. In this respect the readiness of women to develop the skills which help in periods of company growth and development may serve to give them a competitive advantage over their male counterparts.

How Female Entrepreneurs Measure Current Success

The performance of firms was assessed against two sets of criteria. These were quantitative measures of the firm's achievements and qualitative assessments by the respondents. In an emerging area it is useful to allow the respondents to give their personal assessments of the relative performance of their companies and to allow them to determine the criteria upon which to base their judgement. These 'internalized' criteria provide the clues for initiatives to motivate or support actual and potential female entrepreneurs. Respondents were asked two sets of questions. The first dealt with areas in which they believed their firms have achieved success, usually against pre-set personal targets. The second dealt with areas in which they would like their firms to succeed in the future. The personal emphasis upon entrepreneurship and the performance of companies in relation to personal goals were both reflected in the criteria upon which success and failure were judged.

The immediate and the long-term objective of the majority of businesses is to provide independence and personal control. The way this is achieved varied from business to business. In terms of current business performance, most of the respondents judge themselves to be exceptionally successful. Commercial and externally quantifiable measures of performance are seldom considered to be a current priority. This may be attributed to the fact that commercial measures of success are not the immediate objective of most businesses. These were therefore not an initial criteria upon which success was judged.

Surprisingly, cross-sectional analysis by firm age showed no significant difference between new and well-established companies. This indicates that at any given time the majority of businesses in the sample judge business performance against personal goals as opposed to commercial criteria. This apparent anomaly in the results is probably a function of both the small scale of the businesses at the time of investigation and the small sample size.

Commercial measures of business performance are based upon: market position; turnover; profitability; customer service and additional employment created by the firms. As Table 6.1 shows, the commercial criteria generally rated lower as a measure of current success than qualitative measures, with the notable exception of customer service. The large number of citations given to customer service probably reflects two factors. First, small businesses generally take pride in providing a flexible and responsive service for their customers. Second, for women in particular, this aspect of business is emphasized by traditionally female gender roles. An interior designer described it thus:

> ... the client comes first. I know that I can provide an excellent service, one that they wouldn't get from a big firm. I see the designs right through to the end so that I know that my standards will be kept high. I go to their houses and see what they need and see that it is carried through.

The one respondent who felt that her business was unsuccessful at providing a good customer service—a woman who had drifted into business—ceased trading between first and second interview.

Success in terms of employment and jobs was less important. Aspirants and proven achievers placed more emphasis upon additional employment than other groups. This demonstrates their growth orientation. Employment for owners scored higher ratings than employment for staff. This probably reflects the relative newness of the businesses. The motivation that women had for entering business was to provide independence by creating their own careers. This was generally the immediate objective of the business and one in which they had succeeded in achieving. Additional employment was seen as an element which would come later as part of a long-term strategy. As Table 6.1 shows, potential employment achieved significantly higher very successful and successful ratings than actual employment. In fact, employment was relatively high with over 500 jobs created by the 60 firms. The lack of emphasis placed on additional employment as a criterion for success indicates that additional employment is not judged to be an immediate objective for most entrepreneurs.

Finance and income gained was ranked lowest in terms of very successful scores, but achieved a high number of successful and average scores (43) mostly by the achievement-orientated groups. Respondents declined to rate their businesses as very successful against this criteria for

Table 6.1 Upon what criteria do you rate success? How successful have you been in these areas?

	Very success-ful	Success-ful	Average	Unsuccess-ful	Very unsuccess-ful
Independence*	46	8	5	1	0
Customer service†	38	19	2	1	0
Personal satisfac-tion*	37	16	6	1	0
Employment for owner†	30	19	12	1	2
Quality of working life*	26	20	7	5	2
Growth potential†	17	27	12	4	0
Employment for staff†	12	15	22	3	8
Finance/income†	8	22	21	5	4

* Internal quality criteria.
† External commercially quantifiable criteria.
Note: Numbers refer to number of times criteria were cited.

a number of reasons. While some responses could be attributed to modesty, others stated that profitability ratios could always be improved. For the re-entrant and hierarchical groups, however, profitability was not a personal goal but a measure of success imposed by individuals outwith the firm. Thus, success in terms of turnover, profitability and income achieved by the business was often judged more objectively by respondents. Many stated that they were quite happy with the turnover, but wondered how it would be judged by advisers external to the business, such as bank managers and accountants.

The achievement of independence was cited by respondents as their area of greatest success. Similarly, other quality factors, such as personal satisfaction and quality of working life, were also perceived to be criteria against which they had achieved success.

> It's just having complete control over everything within the company. I am like that in all senses, even in my own personal life I like independence. But I think it is just making decisions and sticking by them and deciding and planning for the future. I like all that side of it.

It would appear that the initial motivations and business objectives — the search for independence — are fulfilled by business ownership. Only one woman, a re-entrant, stated that her business, defined in terms of independence, fell below her initial expectations. A high proportion of women stated that personal satisfaction or self-realization was also gained through business ownership.

One young respondent, a social photographer, commented:

> I would get an awful kick out of being well known. If I go to a 'sloane ranger' drinks party and somebody has heard of me because they've seen my photographs in Country Life for that week, I would get a kick out of it. But don't we all like showing off? In the future it would be jolly nice to have a shop front with my name on it.

Although quality of working life was highly rated by most respondents, it was regarded by seven accidentalists as being an area where they had been either unsuccessful or very unsuccessful. Dissatisfaction in this area was directly attributed to the large amount of time respondents had to devote to maintaining the business.

Current performance assessments demonstrate that for the majority of women, current success tends to be measured in terms of personal quality factors as opposed to commercial measures of business performance. They also demonstrate that business ownership fulfilled initial motivations and objectives of independence and personal control.

Measuring Future Success

Distinct differences emerged between the criteria for current and future success in business performance. Table 6.2 shows how respondents,

Table 6.2 Please rank, in order of importance, the areas in which you would like your business to succeed.

	First most important	Second most important	Third most important	Fourth most important
Finance/income*	20	7	12	11
Personal satisfaction†	15	6	7	4
Growth/expansion*	9	10	8	3
Service to customers*	7	12	6	14
Quality of working life†	4	12	8	8
Independence/control†	4	8	6	6
Employment for staff*	1	2	6	7
Employment for self*	0	2	6	1‡

* External commercially quantifiable criteria.
† Internal quality criteria.
‡ Number of times cited.

having achieved the immediate objective of independence, sought to judge the future success of their enterprise against commercial criteria. Cross-sectional analysis by both firm age and by group indicates that this result was in evidence in all the groups and in most of the companies, regardless of the age of the business. Thus, companies which had been in existence for more than 10 years still judged present success against personal criteria, but projected future performance indicators as being commercial criteria. This finding is interesting on two levels. First, it demonstrates that, regardless of the timescale taken to achieve commercially quantifiable success by the different groups, there was a high awareness of the need to fulfil this objective. Second, it is interesting to note that neither the actions nor, among some groups, the desire needed to fulfil this level of success were always in evidence.

Financial issues, in particular, increased in importance. This is probably a function of the fact that entrepreneurs have to ensure the continued existence of the business, and that having achieved personal goals by the very act of entrepreneurial venturing, they seek to enhance the status of the business in terms of external measures of performance. This result was particularly noticeable among aspirants, proven achievers and re-entrants projecting growth.

A lingerie designer and manufacturer explained:

> I would probably relate more to the monetary side, although again, because you are making a five million turnover a year that doesn't mean that you are making a two million pound profit. A lot can be disguised as profits. Some people can get caught up with trying to get a high turnover while not really making a profit.

For most women, especially among the achievement-orientated groups and the returners projecting growth, after individual financial needs had been met, continuing or excess profitability is seen as an external measure of success to be achieved rather than a primary objective for personal gain.

The owner-manager of a market research consultancy explained her attitude towards growth:

> Now I see signs that perhaps the company could really grow, beyond perhaps even my expectations. That is quite exciting and the idea that I could have control over a smallish company with a reasonable turnover, would be very satisfying. It is not something that motivated me in the beginning, but I can see it motivating me as the job progresses.

Factors leading to the growth of the firm also increased in importance but at the expense of employment factors rather than personal satisfaction. As Table 6.2 demonstrates, employment for both self and others ranks considerably lower in future criteria of success than in current success criteria. One woman described her experience of staff planning:

> Just through my own industry and past experiences, when you are busy you have to be really organized, you have got to get the girls working night shifts and things like that. You tend to plan for it more and don't take on more staff because you know you are going to hit a dip again.

Only one woman stated that employment for staff was the most important area of future success for her business. Understandably, employment for self ranked lowest on the given criteria. Having achieved self-employment it ceases to be a major objective and therefore is no longer an area of great importance.

Of the internal quality measures only personal satisfaction was ranked as a priority for future success, providing further evidence that independence and control, while being major objectives at the outset of the business, are fulfilled by business ownership. Having achieved initial ambitions, entrepreneurs focus upon quantitative performance indicators and long-term quality objectives, such as satisfaction and quality of life, for future success.

Few differences emerged between the groups in their assessment of future performance criteria. While this reflects the nature of the classifications, made on the basis of pre-start motivations and experience, it also demonstrates that, regardless of timescale, all respondents desired future business success in terms of conventional commercial criteria. This is supported by the lack of any significant differences by firm age between the groups.

The two success ratings, the first based on individual judgement and current performance, the second based on the desirability of future areas of success, show significant differences. While the first is a subjective self-assessment of business performance, many women stated that when ranking areas of future success they were more objective, rating the business in more conventional terms, as, perhaps, their bank manager would. Thus, the two measures produce quite different results, the first showing areas upon which they have concentrated considering them to be priority areas, the second a more objective assessment of external measures. The differences between the ratings also demonstrate how women, having achieved the immediate—personal—objectives of the business, look to develop their businesses in more conventional terms.

It is likely that the criteria and ranking of current and future performance indicators by the proprietors is linked to the anticipated growth and development of the firm. While distinct differences do appear between the groups in their assessment of current performance criteria, few differences emerge in their assessment of future performance criteria. Nevertheless, the groupings do provide a useful indicator of the likely future development of the companies. It is probable that, unless personal goals change significantly, achievement-orientated groups will develop ventures to their maximum capacity; re-entrants may look to company growth but over an extended timescale; hierarchicals demonstrate characteristics of the typical family business owner who curtails growth after a comfort level has been attained. For accidentalists, change is interesting in as much as they are unlikely and initially unwilling entrepreneurs. For them, growth is a function of changing personal attitudes towards entrepreneurship after direct experience of business ownership.

In conclusion, this study supports earlier propositions that women view proprietorship as a mechanism for achieving independence and control over their working lives. Female entrepreneurs are not, however, an homogeneous group. While classifications for the purpose of analysis may vary, any taxonomy must take account of the dynamic nature of female entrepreneurship and the subsequent effect upon entrepreneurial ventures. Group change is not universal, however, but is most frequently a result of either direct experience of business ownership or a change in personal circumstances.

The results also demonstrate that, among this sample, initial motivations for start-up and experience prior to business ownership did not determine the outcome of the venture. Company growth and development (or in many cases, a lack of growth and development) was more often determined by direct experience of business ownership and personal attitudes towards entrepreneurship at any given time.

CASE STUDY

Company activity:	*Graphic Design Consultancy*
Company started:	*1979*
Employees:	*40*
Business organization:	*Limited Company*

Company History

Together with the other two founding directors of her present company, this respondent left one of the larger, more established graphic design agencies in 1979 to set up her own company. The respondent had been working as a PA administrator to the company chairman, and her position in the newly formed company was mainly concerned with organizational and selling aspects. Her fellow directors were both designers and concentrated on the creative side of the business.

The company now employs 40 people and has an anticipated turnover of £2 million (at 10% profitability) in the next financial year. Due to its rapid growth, shortage of space has been consistently problematic and new premises acquired in the centre of London in 1987 are already too small.

As the company has grown, the respondent has played more of an executive role in the business and until the birth of her second child in late 1987 worked on a part-time basis. More directors have since joined the company and one of the founding members has since died. Consequently, the company has changed dramatically in its first 8 years of operating, as has the role of the respondent. The next major organizational development for the company is likely to be a flotation on the stock exchange.

Start Up

The respondent did not deal with any outside financial institutions during the start-up phase of her business. The £14 000 invested was supplied by the family, friends and personal savings and the respondent does not envisage problems in gaining outside funding should that ever be necessary. Overall, the financial side of her business has posed few problems for the respondent.

Although the respondent had experience in administration, she had little knowledge of the specific skills necessary to successfully start up a new company. She took the LEntA business training course which provided her with a number of the basic skills, although both selling and book-keeping remained difficult for her throughout the early stages of the business development. The respondent emphasized the need for people starting their own business to have business skills.

> I would advise people to make sure that they are very well grounded in the legal basics. If that means taking advice from professional people, then you should do so. That includes very basic things like making sure you are properly insured, covering all the ground work thoroughly. After you've done the ground work and got the product saleable, then it is a question of confidence and belief in yourself that you can do it.

During her first years in business the respondent feels that she did lack confidence, both in her contact with customers and in dealing with a rapidly growing work force. At this time, and throughout the life of the business, she relied heavily on her husband for domestic and moral support. He is not self-employed and has no interest in the business.

> I think personal support is absolutely vital. From a moral point of view, and just getting up, getting out in the morning if you have children, and running the house, and all that. I think it is absolutely necessary, if you are married and have children at home.

A second area of concern for the respondent has been related to the rapid growth in the number of employees working for her company. Very quickly the respondent turned from being an employee into an employer. However, by "watching what was going on, and watching what other people did" the respondent believes that she, and the company, have developed an open management style:

> We tried to establish an open system of management which brings its own problems. But, we always tried to retain a sort of family feel, that we are well known by clients and staff, and to retain that sort of spirit for the company. But it is more difficult with more people.

She is particularly aware of difficulties in dealing with female employees, who make up a large proportion of the professionals working for her company. One problem has been the lack of female support for her ideas about offering progressive maternity leave and other benefits to the female staff.

Growth and Development

The company is growing rapidly, but the expansion is not unmanaged as the respondent and her fellow directors have consciously developed a framework for growth:

> We have got a framework for development and growth. Although it seems we grew out of the framework much more quickly than we had anticipated, and we are growing very much along the lines that we designed. But, it is difficult to know if it is going to stop, and where and when it is going to stop, and whether we will get to a point when we don't want to get any larger. When we reach ideal size if you like—full profitability, happiness and productivity.

For the respondent it has not been the encouragement of growth which has been her focus. She has been concerned about how to manage and adapt to a rapidly developing and expanding business. On a personal level, as the company has grown, the respondent has reassessed her views of the company.

> For a very long time the company was very precious to me. It was part of starting the company up and having been very independent for a long time, it makes it difficult to think of being employed by someone else. Also, for a very long time, I thought the company was my life's work, but I don't know if that is so any more. It could be that being taken over or going to the stock market would allow me to do something else.

For the respondent, it is personal control and independence that are important, rather than control over her company. As a result she intends to leave the company and start again should it go public or be taken over.

> For me it is personal. It is all independence over my own life within the structure I have created. I don't feel I have to be the one that says it is going

to be this, that or the other. For that reason I have now come to the conclusion that I am probably better in start-up situations than I am in big company situations. That sounds contrary but you have more control over a small set up than you have over a large one.

The respondent has not resisted the growth and expansion of her business. Instead she has encouraged its rapid expansion as, she believes, the more successful and profitable she can make this company, then the more capital will be available to her when she moves on to new projects.

7

How Female Entrepreneurs View Failure

Since the mid-1970s there has been a continuous rise in the numbers of people starting in business or turning to self-employment. The lack of national sampling frames makes it difficult to give precise figures of the exact number of people who start trading in any given year. Despite this, data sources such as the Labour Force Surveys and VAT registrations besides Dun and Bradstreet data can give estimates of changes within the small firm sector. New company registrations increased from 69 000 to 115 000 between 1980 and 1986 (Central Statistical Office, 1988) and the number of self-employed people increased from 1.9 million in 1979 to more than 2.9 million in 1987 (Department of Employment, 1988). The increase in business ventures has been well publicized over the previous few years. Only recently has the associated—and inevitable—increase in business failure been given similar attention.

The analysis and interpretation of statistical data from VAT registrations and deregistrations provides small business researchers with probably the most robust source of information on the births and deaths of firms in Britain. This data provides us with an insight into the survival rate of businesses and the turbulence inherent within the small firms sector of the economy.

For all businesses, deaths (or deregistrations) are highest during the first few years of trading, with nearly two-thirds of all failures occurring within the first 30 months of registration. Within this period the times between 6 and 12 months and 12 and 18 months have higher failure rates, indicating times of special vulnerability for all firms (Ganguly and Bannock, 1985). Among sole proprietorships and partnerships, 63% of failures occurred within the first thirty months, 28% in the next 30 months and 9% after 5 years. Companies and incorporated businesses display similar patterns of closure. Nearly a third of all companies which start in business will cease trading within the first 4 years. Between 1980 and 1984 690 000 businesses ceased trading, representing nearly half the total number of companies within the United Kingdom (Foley and Green,

116

1989). It is the smallest firms which are the most vulnerable to periods of economic recession. In support of this, the Quarterly Survey of Small Business in Britain reported that between 1989 and 1990, one-third of the smallest businesses with less than £150 000 turnover shed staff and contracted (Small Business Research Trust, 1990).

Knowledge of the human dimension of business failure is as poorly understood as aggregate data on business failure. Scholars interested in pursuing the issues of business failure and bankruptcy from a qualitative perspective face two major methodological problems. First, the difficulties involved in tracing former business owners ensure that researchers are dependent upon personal knowledge or word of mouth for their main source of contact. Second, business failure is a traumatic experience which often implies a severe reduction in both income and social status for the individual or family involved. Few former owners are keen to participate in research studies. The combination of these two factors leads researchers to depend on incomplete and non-random samples to gain a qualitative insight into business failure.

Business failure is a fundamental issue all too infrequently addressed by researchers of small business and self-employment. But to build a complete picture of self-employment, any research study must address the issues of failure as well as success.

For this study, 10 women were chosen as a subsample to provide case studies of business failure: how it occurred; whether it was preventable; and the human cost involved. Besides these 10 respondents, four women included in the main sample ceased trading between the first and second interview. They were able to recount the process to the research team during the follow-up interview. Two of these companies were new starts who gave up voluntarily after being offered paid employment. Two, however, went into liquidation. Some of their experiences are included in this chapter.

Failure is, in some cases, an inappropriate definition. Six of the sample experienced bankruptcy or traumatic failure; three ceased trading voluntarily before liquidation. The last sold her business as she felt 'no longer in control'. In all cases, the sample had given clear indications of being 'at risk'. They had experienced problems both in starting up and running the business. Some of these problems, especially the inability to raise ongoing finance and their use of unsuitable premises, had been insuperable.

The subsample was as heterogeneous as the main group interviewed (Table 7.1). Aged between 24 and 55, these women had traded in businesses as varied as manufacturing, retailing and estate agency. There was wide diversity in the length of time the businesses had been trading but the average time in existence was 2 years and 9 months.

Table 7.1   Profile of lapsed businesses.

Business activity	Age range	Number of employees	Traded for
Manufacturing furniture	–25	0	1 year 3 months
Haberdashery	26–40	0	1 year 3 months
Private detective	26–40	0	7 months
Manufacturing preserves	41–55	0	1 year 6 months
Retail knitwear	41–55	0	1 year 9 months
Estate agency	26–40	3	2 years 3 months
Retail gifts	26–40	4	5 years
Manufacturing baby clothes	26–40	20	6 years
Cafe/shop	41–55	22	7 years
Publisher	26–40	45	1 year 6 months

This was the first and only experience of business ownership for most. Two had previous experience of ownership, one as a sleeping partner in a family firm, the other had started a retail jewellery outlet but sold the business after trading for 13 weeks. Another respondent had worked as a self-employed outworker for a knitwear firm on a part-time basis to supplement her husband's income before starting her own knitwear shop.

Lack of experience was closely associated with failure. This is especially true when contrasted with the main sample who had previous knowledge of management, business organization or self-employment.

The chosen forms of business organization were sole trader (four), partnership (four) and limited company (two). As with the main sample, companies with limited liability status were older and more established. Five of the businesses traded as retail outlets which, as we see later in this chapter, had implications in terms of capitalization.

In total, the 10 lapsed businesses employed 94 people, not including the owner-managers. The largest employers tended to be in the service sectors such as publishing and catering, although 20 manufacturing jobs were also lost when the businesses closed. All of this subsample tended to lack clearly defined recruitment policies. Only two respondents stated that they preferred female employees and another five said that they looked for specific skills when recruiting employees. Qualifications, work experience and marital status were not significant factors in employee recruitment.

None of the women in this sample could be described as being achievement orientated. Of the women 'returners' in the group, none received the necessary support from their family or spouse. Many also lacked clear, commercial support systems. Overall they lacked clearly defined management styles or business strategies.

Planning in the Lapsed Business

Reasons given for starting in business were varied but the two most cited responses were the desire for independence and the challenge of business ownership, replicating the results of the main sample.

> It was difficult to get an interesting job. I had often thought about self-employment, and thought that I would like to own and have control of my own business and see it through to the end.

> I wasn't being stretched enough. Though I liked the company and I liked the product and being solely responsible for my area. Then I realized that there is more scope if you run the show yourself. There is greater intellectual stimulation.

When interviewed many of the women in this subsample were defensive about their initial motivations for self-employment.

One woman who has since started working for a management consultancy group said:

> I didn't set up the business with any burning desire to get on to the Unlisted Securities Market within 5 years or anything like that. It just seemed like a good idea at the time, and I wanted to do something different. . . . It just worked out that way and it seemed like a good idea at the time.

The combination of *ad hoc* decisions to start up, lack of commercial edge or niche and poor sense of direction was fatal for the business. Experience of management before starting in business was seldom in the commercial policy areas of finance or marketing and only two went on training courses to learn specific business skills whilst preparing to start up.

Experience of business or related disciplines prior to starting in business was limited for many of the women. Five felt that their occupations prior to starting the business was wholly unrelated, and a further three stated that it was only slightly related. Only two women said that their occupations immediately prior to start-up were substantially related to their business.

We can see from Table 7.2 that seven of the 10 respondents were either unemployed or not working immediately prior to starting in business. Some, moreover, had not worked in the formal labour market for several years before start-up. Of the main sample, only 30% were unemployed or not working. It is clear that there may be links between lack of contemporaneous experience in the labour market and subsequent business failure.

There was a perception among these seven women that the lack of paid and relevant employment prior to start-up might have had a detrimental impact upon the new business. One woman who started a retail outlet selling specialist haberdashery products said:

> People have said to me before I started the business, they thought I should have worked in a business for 6 months. I personally didn't go for jobs very much. Maybe it would have been better to have had a job for a year, before I actually started a business of my own. Any job. Especially if you haven't worked for a while.

An unwillingness to learn from others or invest in preparation was common. A woman who took over an estate agency as a going concern commented:

> When I first started this I didn't know anybody in estate agents or housing associations or lettings . . . somebody suggested that I should have worked in a company for 6 months, I probably should have done, but you may feel that you are getting on and you don't want to waste time. But you must not think like that.

The period between initial consideration of the idea and business launch varied considerably. Two respondents had planned the business for less than 1 month before starting. A further five had taken up to 6 months. Three had taken up to 2 years in the planning stage. Six of these respondents said that they had planned the business in their spare time but only four of all the lapsed businesses had written a business plan. This contrasts with the very high proportion of survivors and successes who formally planned.

Precipitous market entry was common. Nine of the subsample had started trading on a full-time basis rather than 'testing the market' before full launch. One woman who had started trading on a full-time basis explained that she had not undertaken any market research whilst preparing the business. She thought that any deficiencies in her idea could be resolved after the start-up.

Table 7.2   Occupation prior to start-up.

Occupation	No.
Senior management	1
Secretarial (clerical)	1
Manual	0
Not employed (housewife)	3
Unemployed	4
Self-employed (part time)	1
Total	10

Table 7.3 Problems experienced (lapsed businesses).

Problem areas	Any problems	Most serious problem
Late payment of bills	5	4
Finding business/clients	5	3
Other cash flow problems	5	2
Undercharging for product	4	
Getting advice	3	
Finding premises	2	
VAT on unpaid bills	2	
Effect on personal life	2	
Understanding marketing	2	
Employing staff	1	
Book-keeping	1	
Understanding VAT/tax/NI	—	
Regulations/form filling	—	

We had more or less looked into everything. We had got an accountant and everything, so I thought well, you can get them to advise you. It is not until after you are in and you start it you see the pitfalls, and you begin to wonder if you have done the right thing. But then you carry on regardless.

The Impact of External Barriers

This group of women experienced a wide ranging variety of anxieties before starting in business. As in the main sample, all the respondents in this group display a great deal of concern with the financial aspects of business ownership. Finding clients and customers and the impact of government regulations were also cited as major areas of concern. This preoccupation with inputs rather than outputs may give some insight into their ways of managing. Their problems generally, with the notable exception of premises, reflected many of the areas which the respondents later cited as problematic and ultimately leading to the demise of the business.

The respondents described experiences which were similar to the problems encountered by the main sample, mainly cash flow and finding clients (Table 7.3). Unlike the main sample, none of the lapsed businesses had developed strategies to overcome problems.

All the businesses survived long enough for anxieties about government regulations to be abandoned in favour of the more immediate problems of marketing and cash flow. All respondents cited at least one financial aspect of the business as being problematic. Three problems were perceived as being exacerbated by gender: late payment of bills by customers, finding clients and getting advice and information.

Only one respondent cited childcare arrangements as a major problem. This, however, proved serious enough for her to abandon self-employment in favour of a paid job:

> ... the reasons why I decided to come out and work for a bigger organization were that with my husband away and having the kids to manage and the house to run and everything else, actually physically having the energy and motivation to devote to building up the business, really just wasn't there. I just couldn't do it. The other thing about (working for) this organization was, when I came here the attitude that they took to the fact that I was a woman who had children was so totally different from any other experience that I've had in my working life that I was quite stunned by it ... their attitude is very positive: "good on you for trying to do what you are doing, we'll help you where we can". It is very, very difficult working with two small children anyway but it is made a bit easier by their attitude.

Other women found the lack of domestic support a major burden in two ways. First, they often had to complete their usual household tasks by themselves in addition to running the business. Second, support by their domestic partners in the day-to-day running of the business was not forthcoming. One woman described her husband's attitude:

> Well, he kind of left me to it. He didn't interfere. He helped us in the shop doing things, all the electrical work in the shop and everything, but he just sort of left us and didn't interfere and say "oh, you should be doing that or you should be doing this". I think I was more independent. Maybe that is where I went wrong. Maybe I should have asked for his help. ... I don't think he would have known, he didn't know anything about wool or anything like that.

Another respondent who was subsequently offered employment with an international firm of management consultants described her domestic problems differently:

> My problem wasn't that I was a woman. My problem was that Chris [her husband] wasn't there. You could sort of say that I am a single parent Monday to Friday, in that sense, because I had the responsibility for everything. But if Chris had been there, that would have been different, because in many ways he does more of that type of stuff than I ever do. I think that it was a function of the fact that I was on my own, rather than a function of the fact that I was a woman.

Despite the last respondent's analysis, many of the problems facing women in business are gender related. Many women in this group accented negative, traditional views of their capabilities often offered by their own families, and many were unable to restructure their domestic arrangements or exploit their assets. In this sense, women in business have a definite disadvantage when compared with their male counterparts. Evidence from other studies looking at male business ownership suggests that 'contributing wives' are a major source of often unpaid labour in their husbands' firms (Scase and Goffee, 1980, 1982; Kirkham, 1987). This study demonstrates that few women can expect support in the form of a working contribution from their domestic partners. Commonly cited problems such as childcare provision and lack of domestic support have an obvious gender dimension. Other barriers such as capitalization, finding clients and undercharging for products or services can have a more insidious gender dimension.

Female owner-managers both perceive and experience difficulties with apparently straightforward (and apparently non-gender-related) tasks such as getting business and finding clients. This makes the task of a female business owner even more difficult than her male counterparts and has implications for the long-term success of any venture started by a woman. As the main sample has shown, specific strategies often have to be developed in order to overcome these problems. In this subsample of lapsed businesses, few were able to do so.

Two problems, capitalization and the acquisition and usage of business premises, seemed to be of particular importance for these ten businesses and will be examined in depth.

Finance

The amount of start-up capital initially invested in the businesses varied widely (Table 7.4). At the two extremes, one woman, who developed from designer to manufacturer of baby clothes, started her business at home on a part-time basis, using only her husband's salary for initial investment. Another woman, who started publishing trade directories, invested £110 000 in addition to an overdraft facility of £50 000.

Sources of finance also varied. Four respondents had relied upon institutional sources, financing their businesses with bank loans and overdrafts. Others had been financed by their families, personal savings and inheritance. In one case, the respondent, financing her business solely by personal savings, did not approach a bank until the savings had been used up. Finance was then denied, the respondent saying that the bank manager "believed we were just women doing women's things".

Table 7.4   Start-up capital (lapsed businesses).

Capital invested	No. of businesses
None	1
Less than £1000	1
£2000−£4999	2
£5000−£9999	2
£10 000−£19 999	1
£20 000−£50 000	2
More than £50 000	1
Total	10

Four respondents had been asked to provide security to offset bank lending and in one case this security was taken up when the business closed. All of the women in this group experienced personal financial difficulties as a result of business failure.

Eight of the women stated that the initial investment was not sufficient to capitalize their businesses, but this was only supplemented in three cases. Of the remaining five, three women sought but were denied further finance and two decided at that point to cut their losses and close the business.

Problems raising start-up capital were seldom resolved and few went on to develop normal business relationships with their bank managers. Most preferred to "let the business speak for itself" and poor relations with bankers were common. In a few of the businesses, communications deteriorated to such an extent that relations collapsed completely with virtually no interaction and daily business could not commence. The women complained that banks refused them any overdraft facilities for the day-to-day running of the business and often refused to honour cheques without advance notice. As several of the women noted, the bankers seemed to expect the business to fail and acted to minimize their own risks.

Few respondents in this subsample developed business strategies to deal with professionals such as bankers and accountants. Respondents complained of patronizing behaviour and attitudes towards them. This in turn made it difficult for them to establish good working relationships. Many of the women stated that their overriding impressions of bank managers were that they treated female clients as "women doing men's work", another added that she was made to feel like a "silly child" by her male bank manager. A former manufacturer of baby clothes described her relationship with her financial advisers:

The accountant was very antagonistic. The director of the accountancy firm was downright rude—he even accused me of stealing from the company and he said that I was inept. He was even worse than the bank manager who was just plain patronizing. He was very awkward when I went to open a business account, he would not let me because I had no capital and so I ended up opening another personal account.

After closing the business which employed 20 people, her bank manager remarked that she: "was the first woman they'd ever lent money to and on your record you'll be the last". Failure, in this case, was directly attributed to gender by the banker.

Financial problems were not restricted to capitalization of the business. One respondent stated that the lack of a secure income throughout the life of the business was partially responsible for her closing down.

> The money wasn't the overriding concern, but it was a pretty big concern by that time. . . . I think there is an underestimated stress in not having a secure salary. At first you think, oh well, it will be alright. I did kind of make enough money to get along with, but there is always that nagging doubt at the back of your mind that you are not going to make enough the next month. That I think is quite massively underestimated.

Surprisingly, neither bad debt nor late payments were put forward as causes of failure. This contrasts with the causes of traumatic failure identified in more traditional non-gender studies.

Premises

Compared with the main sample this group invested a significantly higher proportion of start-up capital on buying, converting or renting premises. Only two of the respondents started their businesses at home, gradually building the business until it could support high overheads. Of the eight who started in external premises, many attributed the demise of the business to the property factor, often citing the fact that capital needed in the daily running of the business was tied up in the high overheads arising from long leases, rent and rates. This was especially noticeable among the retail businesses often ineligible for assistance such as regional development grants and employment assistance schemes.

One respondent, the former owner of a retail outlet selling knitwear, described her experience:

> If I had known, I would never have bothered with a shop. I would have just started up here, and gone from there into a unit and then worked from there, I would never have had a shop at all. I thought you would have to

have a sort of retail business, so that the public can see it. But I have found now that you don't have to have that. By going to exhibitions you don't have to have a shop ... that is how you make your name, by going to exhibitions. Obviously, it cost us a lot of money to find out that you don't need a shop.

This respondent found the time involved with maintaining external premises burdensome as well as the high overheads.

I couldn't get doing any designing myself because I had to keep the shop open. It wasn't really looked into enough, I should have thought of that to begin with. But the way it was I couldn't keep up with the orders in the shop, and do my own ... it was just too much.

Having closed her shop because of the costs, she found that she continued paying rent and rates after she had moved out.

... you can't just shut up shop and walk out you see. I got in touch with the wool companies and asked if they would take the yarn back, most of them were quite good and they did. We still owe small amounts to some of them. We try and pay it off naturally, but the worst thing of the lot was the rent. If he [her accountant] had said to us, pay your rent and stay on and have a big sale it would have been okay, but he didn't he told us to shut the shop and get out. My husband had to pay up two thousand pounds for rent and we weren't even in the shop, then we got a rates bill for twelve hundred pounds ... we have got to pay it. We have no choice. If we don't pay it we could go to gaol. What do you do?

Other respondents also found their choice of retail outlets was poor:

I think one of the main problems that I faced was the fact that the shop was badly located. It was not on a main road, so you weren't getting passing traffic. It was in a lane, it was a very nice little arcade, but because it was off the beaten track there were a lot of people in the area who didn't know it was there. I think really a great deal more marketing could have been done on a large scale beyond just the group advertising that we were doing ourselves. The lane got into such a state of disrepair that it was getting very, very difficult for people to get there.

Both respondents quoted above started, in retrospect they realized unnecessarily, in retail units. Both women now recognize that the cost of keeping a retail outlet placed burdensome costs upon their businesses. Both feel that businesses could have survived had they started at home, exhibiting and selling through organized trade fairs and progressing, as necessary, into low cost workspace.

Table 7.5 From whom did you seek advice? Were they helpful?

Adviser	Pre-start		Start-up		Ongoing	
	Helpful	Unhelpful	Helpful	Unhelpful	Helpful	Unhelpful
Bank	3	0	4	1	3	1
Solicitor	3	0	4	0	1	0
Accountant	2	1	5	0	3	1
Family	1	1	1	0	1	1
Friends	0	0	0	1	3	0
Enterprise agency	0	1	0	1	1	2
Local authority	0	0	0	0	2	0
Small Firms Service	1	0	0	0	0	0

It is clear from this small sample that the decision to locate in external premises is fundamental to the long-term viability of any small business. It would appear that this is especially so for the retail sector. Problems experienced in this subsample include long leases, high rates and inappropriate locations. While in-depth market research can resolve locational problems, others can only be resolved by the widespread availability of suitable small business workspaces with 'easy-in easy-out' options to suit the often vulnerable new firm.

Advice and Assistance in the Lapsed Firm

Many of the respondents complained about the quality of advice and assistance available to them. Most had sought advice at one stage or another, six at the pre-start phase, but only five during the start-up and ongoing periods of their businesses (Table 7.5). As in the main sample, sources of advice varied as much as the perceived quality, as Table 7.5 demonstrates. The most commonly used advisers remained banks, solicitors and accountants, reflecting also the preference of the main sample, and there was general satisfaction with the help given by these groups of professionals. Only one woman had contacted a local enterprise agency during the pre-start and start-up phase of business and had found the advice unhelpful. The women were generally ambivalent about the informal advice given by friends and family, with as many stating that it was unhelpful as there were those who appreciated this largely unsolicited help.

Although five respondents said that they had an informal network of contacts that they could use for advice, only two women were members of employers associations or business clubs. One woman found even joining networks difficult.

> Well actually, I phoned those people from Battersea, to try to get information about that business club, and I phoned up a number of times and they were always busy. They always used to take my number. So, I gave up in the end. I don't know if that would have helped.

Perhaps because of the lack of business or employment experience among this group, there were cases of excessive dependence upon professionals and, perhaps, unrealistic expectations of their knowledge and the advice that they were prepared to give. One woman complained about her former accountant who she felt had given her inappropriate advice when closing the business.

> I phoned him up this morning and I said to him "We have taken advice from you and I'm after getting a rates bill in, and you must pay it for the first 3 months after you are out of the shop". "The first 3 months", he said, "I was not aware of that". I said: "Well, I think you should have found that out". He should have known all these things. You know, he is an accountant. He is there to tell you these things. I said, "well, actually I am quite annoyed because the advice you gave us has just landed us in more trouble. I have had the Sheriff Officers up at my door and everything, you told me that the house was in my husband's name, I didn't have to worry about anything, but what you didn't tell me was the fact that I would have to prove what was my husband's. Anything else that was in the house that I didn't have a receipt for or my husband's name on it they could take. They could empty my wardrobes, they told me. They could empty everything out of the house. Anything, maybe the suite which we didn't have a receipt for, they could take that away ...".

Having closed that business the respondent was intent upon staying self-employed "to pay off debts from the last business". She was then asked where she would go to seek advice in her new venture.

> To be honest, I don't really know where to go, that is the truth. I don't really know where to start. I don't see any sense in going back to the SDA, because all they will tell me is, go and get a loan, find a workshop or something like that. So I don't really see any sense in going to them again. I honestly don't think they are really interested in you unless you are on the 'bru', signing on and getting money. I don't really think that they are interested in married women starting up on their own, because you are not taking somebody off

the unemployment list. They don't care. If it was a young person unemployed and getting money every week, then they would get help. But, I think because you are a woman and you are not registered, I don't think they are interested.

Management Strategies in the Lapsed Firm

As we have seen from previous chapters, strategies in overcoming problems are, for many female entrepreneurs, the key to market success. In the case of the 10 women who had ceased trading, none had developed consistent or coherent strategies to overcome barriers to business ownership or problems faced once in business. This was a major factor in their market failure.

Especially noticeable was the lack of any previous experience in business, management or in many cases recent employment. None of the women lacking in recent employment experience sought to redress this. Only two women recognized that this lack of experience could materially affect their chances of business success and sought training in business ownership and management prior to starting the business. This can be contrasted with the main sample, many of whom had management experience but still undertook further training to compensate for any deficiencies that remained. For the main sample the acquisition of training was a major strategy. In this subsample of business failures, it was noticeably lacking.

The former owner of a restaurant described her experiences of business management:

> I didn't know about proper controls. We should have looked at the turnover profit margin—I wasn't aware of this. There wasn't sufficient quality control. The cost of goods and preparation of the finished meal wasn't calculated and we should have paid more attention to cash flow. It was a textbook example of how not to manage a restaurant, because each and every director went off and did something else, myself included. I was looking after the children and running the shop. The staff more or less got left to run the business, at which point there were no controls, and they wished to form a collective in order to attempt to take over the business, couldn't get the money together and the whole thing descended into rather a maelstrom, is the only way I can describe it. It went downhill. If there are no limits then it is not your business, then staff take advantage and obviously the business ends up having no direction anymore and that is precisely what happened.

Other women also described problems in managing staff, as a former estate agent explained:

When times were slack and there was nothing to do in the office then we would all sit around and talk to each other, one to one. Then, of course, it became difficult for me to actually be the boss and assert myself if they did anything wrong. Really, I was too soft. People often say that about me. In fact, my solicitor actually said to one of my customers "she will really have to go at it if she wants to succeed".

Formal and informal networking was also conspicuous by its absence. None of the subsample were aware of the opportunities offered by informal networking in testing markets and gaining free and relevant advice. Only two were members of formal business organizations or networks throughout the life of the business. Even where women were members of business organizations there was a sense of diffidence and a reluctance to get involved in the groups. None of these women were able to gain potential clients and buyers into the business by using either established or self-made networks of contacts.

A common strategy used by the main group, de-personalization, was not used by this group. This could reflect two factors. First, few of these women wanted their lives or personalities to be changed in any major way by the business. Second, the businesses in this group were biased towards traditionally female sectors and had not reached the level of sophistication where such a strategy might be used. A more direct strategy of confrontation was not considered appropriate; few were able to identify any experience of direct or indirect discrimination.

This group generally were ambivalent about the idea of business ownership, although whether this came about prior to their experience or after is difficult to determine using *ex-post facto* research methods. Many certainly seemed to lack the persistence and skill necessary to overcome the multiple problems facing women going into business.

Where To Now?

A question asked of these women concerned their future ambitions: would they consider self-employment again? Would they seek employment elsewhere or would the majority return to their previous occupation of housewife? For the seven women who had entered into self-employment from a non-employed status, the initial motivation was to gain a degree of independence coupled with a self-earned income. The business venture had been an expensive exercise both emotionally and financially. Their ambitions for the future, however, were still largely governed by their business experience. Some of the women interviewed stated that they would return to self-employment, albeit in different circumstances, as it was still seen as the ideal form of work for their lives. Two women were in the less fortunate position of perceiving that self-employment was their only means to an income and unwillingly remained self-employed only to service previous business debts. One woman, the former owner of the knitwear shop, is currently in the process of starting another business.

> Yes. I'll stay self-employed. I have no choice really, I've got to keep working to pay the bills.

> I am more disillusioned with the accountant, and the help and advice I got than anything else. Not about going into business, not that at all. Because I enjoy it. That is something that I really enjoy doing. Even if I went into business and it wasn't a success, well I have done it because I wanted to and that's it. It is something that I achieved myself. I would like it to be a success, but if, by chance, it is not, well there is nothing I can do about it.

Half the women felt that they had learnt a great deal about 'good business practice' from their experiences of self-employment and were sure that their future ventures would benefit from this experience.

> Yes. I mean when the bills are paid off and the girls are no longer reliant on me for being there, because that's what it's all about when you are bringing up children. I will probably do my market research better, though the trouble is the risks aren't only in money, but to your whole basic family structure. If you were much more independent, didn't have dependants or have somebody help with those dependants then it's much easier.

> I just wasn't ready for it. I wasn't mature enough to handle being self-employed. My choice of partner was very bad. It was a disaster really, but good experience. I think the main difference is maturity. I feel perfectly capable of doing what I am setting out to do now. Whereas before it didn't even occur to me that I should be acquiring certain skills.

In conclusion, this subsample of women whose businesses have ceased trading are distinguished by their lack of recent experience of the labour market generally, and of business ownership and management in particular, prior to start-up. This may have important implications for their ability to start and manage a business successfully. When compared to the main sample of successful businesses, many of whom also lacked previous direct experience of business ownership, it may be seen that the lack of recent labour market experience has a more important bearing on the ability to sustain a business. Many women in this subsample believed that self-employment had been a useful learning tool for future attempts at business. Prior business failure as a learning experience for future business success is a concept more commonly found in North America than in Britain. It is probable that if these women return to business ownership, extensive additional training in business and management skills would need to be acquired before success is attained.

CASE STUDY

Company activity: *Design and Manufacture of Baby Products and Gifts*
Company traded for: *6 years*
Employees: *22*
Business organization: *Limited Company*

Company History

This respondent set up a manufacturing firm in her home which was successful for a number of years. This firm was then run down and another set up almost immediately. The respondent comes from a background of self-employment. Her father has owned his own company for several years. He took over a quilting business and called upon his daughter's assistance during the purchasing negotiations. The respondent says she learnt a great deal from taking part in this.

The respondent's original firm started in 1980 after the birth of her daughter. The respondent wanted to go back to work immediately and as this proved impossible she began designing and making products from home. One of the first things she designed was a nappy changing bag. It was based on an idea which evolved from discussions with a friend who thought it would be a useful device. This was intended to be a one-off product, like the others the respondent had created, specifically to fit the needs of friends. This product became very popular with all her friends and she made several which she gave away before she realized that she had hit upon a possible business idea. She quickly built a reputation by word of mouth, through calling into nursery shops and showing her product. She also began to attend trade shows and approached the design council. At this stage, she had defined her own strength, and that of the business as to the ability to come up with original and practical designs. By 1984 demand for the nappy changing bag was increasing and it was clear that she had to decide where the business was going as she had far more products and orders than she could cope with. She had begun employing people to produce the nappy bags, all women who worked from home. Her business though still lacked direction and control so she sought help from a local enterprise agency. They recommended that she participated in a new enterprise programme. She qualified for a loan but only on the condition that she employ more staff.

Barriers and Strategies for Success

This respondent was very dissatisfied with the advice given to her whilst on the programme. Her major criticism of them is that their own interests in small businesses is in how many people they employ. This emphasis on job creation forced the respondent to take on more staff than she could cope with. It also resulted in a change of direction for the whole company away from design towards manufacturing. Her financial problems grew. Since she was the biggest single creditor in her own company they were personal as well as business financial problems. This respondent was dissatisfied with her accountancy firm. She went to them for advice when she took out the loan. When the company got into financial difficulty she went back to them and according to her, experienced discrimination and harassment:

> The accountant was very antagonistic. The director of the accountancy firm was downright rude—he even accused me of stealing from the company and he said that I was inept. He was even worse than the bank manager who was just plain patronizing. He was very awkward when I went to open a business account. He would not let me because I had no capital and so I ended up opening another personal account.

Quite soon after this the company went into voluntary liquidation, for a variety of reasons. The final blow was the late payment of bills by her largest customer. This, on top of the additional cost of extra staff, proved too much for the company. Far from being discouraged, however, the respondent set up another company almost immediately. She thinks she has learnt a great deal from her previous experience, in particular the importance of believing in, and carrying out her own business ideas, rather than to assume that a 'professional' advisor always knows best. The present company focuses more on design than manufacturing, which was the respondent's original plan for the first company.

8

Female Entrepreneurship and Family Support

The family emerges in this study as a major influence on: attitudes to business ownership; the development of the venture; and the view female entrepreneurs took of their enterprise. In this chapter the influence of the family upon both the entrepreneurial decision and the ability to build the business beyond the start up stage is examined. Several of the women in the sample were at an age when the influence and support of parents were, if not necessary, then at the least important and desirable. For other women the role of husbands or domestic partners and children were important. As Table 8.1 demonstrates, the majority of respondents were between 26 and 40 years of age and had started their business within the past 5 years. Most of the 13 women who were under 25 years old had started trading within the previous 2 years. The results of the General Household Survey (Curran *et al.*, 1987), show a comparable proportion of self-employed women within the medial age ranges, but also demonstrate the skew in the present sample towards younger women and away from the older age ranges.

The marital status of the respondents also differed in some ways from results of the General Household Survey (Table 8.2). A large proportion of the sample were either married (27) or in a stable relationship (13). Of the remaining 20, 12 were single, six were divorced, one separated and one

Table 8.1   Age of respondents and age of businesses.

| Concerns | Business age | | |
	<1 year No.	1–5 years No.	>5 years No.
Under 25	6	7	0
26–40	7	19	6
41–55	5	4	4
Over 55	0	0	2
Total	18	30	12

Table 8.2   Marital status of respondents.

	Business age		
Concerns	<1 year No.	1–5 years No.	>5 years No.
Single	3	8	1
Married	8	12	7
Stable relationship	5	6	2
Divorced	2	3	1
Separated	0	1	0
Widowed	0	0	1
Total	18	30	12

widowed. While the General Household Survey also reports a high number of married women (75%), differences do occur among the other groups. In particular, there is a significantly higher occurrence of single and divorced women and fewer widows than reported by the General Household Survey. Similar studies of female entrepreneurs have also noted a higher incidence of divorcees than found in the General Household Survey analysis (cf. Goffee and Scase, 1985; Watkins and Watkins, 1986). While Curran (1986) associates this with non-random sampling techniques, the now frequently found incidence of divorcees in independent studies, with no deliberate skew of marital status, makes this a point worth exploring.

Previous studies of both male and female entrepreneurs have examined the role of families, especially parents, in the decision to become self-employed (Kimives, 1974; Litvak and Maule, 1974; Mancuso, 1984; Watkins and Watkins, 1986). Researchers have frequently found that business owners often come from families where parents were themselves either self-employed or had a history of self-employment. In the USA, the percentage of (male) entrepreneurs found to have self-employed fathers or mothers is often cited as being in excess of 50%, with some studies quoting 70% (Kimives, 1974; Mancuso, 1984). In Britain, the issue of paternal influences on career decisions pertaining to self-employment has stimulated similar interest among small business researchers. Few, however, have looked at either the role of paternal influence over female entrepreneurs or, indeed, the links which may exist between maternal occupations and the entrepreneurial activity of daughters. Watkins and Watkins (1986) were the first British researchers who investigated possible linkages. They found that 37% of their sample had fathers who had run a business of their own or were otherwise self-employed and 16% of the mothers of respondents had an independent history of self-employment or business ownership. They concluded that:

> ... a female entrepreneur is some four times more likely to have been subject to the influence of an entrepreneurial parent (father and/or mother) than a member of the general population ... The small numbers involved do not permit us to form a view on the relative importance of a male versus a female entrepreneurial role model. However, the figures do demonstrate that a maternal role model can have at least as great an influence as a paternal one.

Respondents in the present study were asked a series of questions relating to the current and prior employment experience of their parents, siblings and wider family. Given the weight of previous evidence relating to parental influence in what has come to be seen as the 'inheritance of an entrepreneurial tradition', the number of respondents whose parents were currently, or had been, self-employed was found to be lower than anticipated; 13 respondents stated that one of their parents had been self-employed or owned their own business and all were still engaged in that activity (Table 8.3). Thus, the results of this study do not necessarily uphold previous results regarding a direct linkage between parents and offspring in the entrepreneurial decision.

It seems that the influence of the family in decisions regarding occupation is more intricate and complex than is indicated by previous research. For example, it is probable that family members could exert a negative effect upon plans for business ownership; it is also probable that close family members, other than parents, influence career and occupational decisions; it is also likely that proximity to other family businesses not necessarily owned by parents may be an influence, as, of course, could the success or failure of these businesses.

A larger number of respondents had a connection with small business ownership or self-employment from siblings than parents. The respondents cited a total of 61 businesses owned by members of their immediate

Table 8.3 Current employment status of parents.

	Mother		Father	
	No.	%	No.	%
Employed	14	23	16	27
Self-employed	6	10	7	12
Unemployed	9	15	2	3
Retired	22	37	14	23
Deceased	9	15	21	35

Table 8.4 Have any of your family ever started or run their own business?

	Businesses mentioned					
	First business		Second business		Third business	
	No.	%	No.	%	No.	%
Yes, close family* (with employees)	23	38	11	58	2	33
Yes, close family (no employees)	16	27	5	26	4	66
Total, close families	39	65	16	84	6	100
Yes, other family† (with employees)	3	5	1	5	0	0
Yes, other family (no employees)	2	3	2	11	0	0
Total, other families	5	8	3	16	0	0
No	16	27	0	0	0	0
Total	60	100	19	100	6	100

* Parents, siblings.
† Aunts, uncles, cousins.

families and a further eight owned by their extended family (Table 8.4). Of the businesses cited, 43 were described as very successful, 22 as moderately successful and only four described as not successful (Table 8.5). From these results it is possible to conclude that family influence to start in business can stem as much from sisters and brothers as by the much cited 'inheritance of an entrepreneurial culture' from parents.

Table 8.5 How successful was the business?

	First business No.	Second business No.	Third business No.
Very successful	26	11	6
Moderately successful	14	8	0
Not successful	4	0	0
Total	44	19	6

The reaction of families to plans of business ownership has an important impact upon the women. In some cases, it shaped the future prosperity of businesses. For many women, the conflicts which they experienced in establishing themselves as proprietors were related to conflicting roles of wife and mother and businesswoman. The attitudes held by both family and business institutions proved problematic for many women and tended to undermine both the confidence and the credibility of the respondents.

The attitudes of families, perceived as being of great importance in starting up, towards plans of business ownership varied substantially. The respondents recognized that attitudes of families or domestic partners were of crucial importance to the start-up decision. Many women experienced family doubts and disapproval. For them, problems of conflicting roles were unresolved and often unresolvable. One woman in the process of starting up described the conflict:

> Its my in-laws you want to hear about . . . they say that there is no market and that I wouldn't make any money out of it. I really feel that it goes deeper than that. I think it's because they think I shouldn't be doing that and taking out a business loan when I should be trying to have a baby. That's principally what it is. I also feel that they don't think it's fair to Alan to be taking a risk like that . . . but most of all what is behind it is that I am their only chance of having grandchildren because my husband is their only son, and I think that they feel that I should be concentrating on that.

Others, however, were offered a great deal of family support, which they were aware contributed greatly to their personal confidence. A mother and daughter partnership selling wholesale first aid supplies received encouragement from their domestic partners:

> My father and husband are very good. They do give us support and everything, but they don't take it too seriously. I don't think they appreciate how well we are doing—to outsiders we are doing exceptionally well. I think they take it for granted, how well we are doing. But, at the same time, if I come in and say "we have got a really good order with a builders", I'll get a pat on the back and they'll say, "well done, that's really good".

> They keep saying that it's exactly up my street and that I'd be very good at it. If it wasn't for them giving me this support, I might have wavered [freelance copy writer].

> The family I believe is one of the most important things you can have, because there have been times when I've had to work say, 7 days, we didn't go home at all, we worked 24 hours. My mother would come here, she doesn't mind leaving her job to stay with me all night, to meet the particular

order. My sisters, as you can see, will come here and work and the family has been the most important thing in my business so far. You can't do it all by yourself [textile designer].

I feel very alone because I don't have any brothers or sisters and I don't have any parents and that is really very hard when you have to do it all completely on your own. I suppose you could put up with it if you knew there was somebody who you knew would fish you out, if the worst came to the worst. I suppose it is a lack of confidence as well, the fact that you are not going to be able to do it [secretarial services agency].

There were wide variations in the effects of business ownership upon personal and domestic lives.

One third of the sample stated that proprietorship had a detrimental effect upon personal lives. Others stated that business ownership had improved their lives and personal relationships. Three particular areas were examined in this study: relationships with spouse or domestic partners; motherhood; and the general quality of life.

Spouse Relationships

The issue of whether and how personal relationships with spouses had been affected, either positively or negatively, by business ownership was of special interest. Previous studies of the lives of entrepreneurs have demonstrated that male business owners can expect a great deal of, mostly unpaid, business and domestic support from 'contributing wives' (Scase and Goffee, 1982). Female business owners, however, cannot rely on their spouses for the same support and consequently have to assume the full burden of both business and domestic commitments (Goffee and Scase, 1985; Kirkham, 1987). These results were confirmed by this study and it was anticipated, therefore, that the tensions brought about by this situation would lead to a marked deterioration in spouse relationships. However, a surprisingly small proportion stated that spouse relationships had worsened since becoming business owners (Table 8.6). More felt that their relationships had improved. Married women were the least likely to have suffered in terms of personal circumstances since becoming business owners. This result was unexpected but may be explained by a number of factors. First, many married respondents were second wage earners in their households, providing they minimized risk and adopted an 'income substitution' approach they were under less pressure to succeed financially than either single parents or single women.

Table 8.6   Has going into business on your own improved or deteriorated your:

	Relationship with spouse		Relationship with children		Relationship with friends	
	No.	%	No.	%	No.	%
Better	19	32	12	20	12	20
Worse	11	18	5	8	23	38
No difference	15	25	11	18	25	42
Don't know	0	0	0	0	0	0
Not applicable	15	25	32	54	0	0
Total	60	100	60	100	60	100

> In my case the second income earner allowed me to be more relaxed, to develop good ideas. You can chat about it, generally, and follow up hair-brained ideas because it's not quite so vital that it's financially successful.

This can be contrasted with the experiences of a single parent interviewed:

> The trouble is the risks aren't only in money, but to your whole basic family structure. If I were much more independent, didn't have dependants, or if I had somebody who could help with those dependants, it would have been much easier. I could have sold my house, but because I am a single parent and the girls are really happy here, I just feel that I could not deprive them of it.

Many married women, in particular those returning to economic activity, organized their businesses around their husbands and families. As long as the family was the clear priority, conflict between family and business affairs was minimized.

> Anything that I have committed myself to do for the children I always regard as sacrosanct and very rarely will I let them down in any way. So if there is something on, a special day or a school meeting or a birthday and I have promised that I will be there, I will be there. It is not too difficult . . . it is really a matter of muddling through the best that I can. But I will put meetings off if necessary . . . They come first.

> I think that if we found that as a family we were growing apart because we hadn't got a lot of time together I would have to reorganize myself. If I found that as a family we needed more time together, I think both my husband and myself would make sacrifices as far as working was concerned. Your actual personal life it has to take precedence. Working comes second to me. At the moment my husband likes it as it is, he likes to have an intelligent conversation in the evening. Its certainly done our marriage an awful lot of

good being able to compare notes in the evening and generally talk together as intelligent beings.

Finally, the moral support provided by spouses was identified by many respondents as a major asset. As one woman stated:

I think going into business would have been impossible without support from Andy. If there had been an obstacle like a husband who wasn't prepared to help out, or even encourage me a little bit, then I would not have done it.

Others echoed this sentiment:

I think personal support is absolutely vital. From a moral point of view and just getting up, getting out in the morning if you have children, and running the house and all that. I think it is absolutely necessary, if you are married and have children at home.

I do feel if you have a strong sort of family or a permanent person around who supports what you are doing, it just makes all the difference and I think if people can have it, it is marvellous. It doesn't necessarily mean that it has to be a set up like a 'wifey' set-up, it probably needs to be someone who is not actually out to directly compete with you, which is where I think the problems start.

For the respondents whose spouse relationships had deteriorated, lack of time was the most commonly cited cause. Others cited the lack of support which they had received from husbands or domestic partners. One woman, the owner of a women-only gym, experiencing domestic conflict because of the time taken up by proprietorship, had been forced to decide between proprietorship and her husband and child. For this woman the choice had been clear: she chose proprietorship. Other women also experienced this conflict:

Starting in business was not the only reason the relationship broke up, but it was the dominant factor. It was all to do with inequality, it was to do with the fact that, when I was going out with guys we were in very equal positions, financially and status wise, how our friends saw us. That changed dramatically, we were both students when we met, when he became unemployed I started running this company and it was quite an extreme situation.

I was low about 6 months ago, I must admit. I was going out with somebody and it was coming to an end, I did feel that I didn't have the impetus to go on. Now that my new boyfriend is around, he is self-employed too, that has helped an awful lot. We can bounce ideas off each other. I think that you have got to have somebody close to you that has been in business on their own, because other people just do not understand.

Another respondent, a literary agent who had been in business for several years, explained that she found her age (72 years) beneficial, as she no longer worried about her family conflicting with the pressure of work:

> When you are older you don't have the interests that young people have. I have dedicated myself and I work probably 16 hours a day. When you are younger you don't want to do that, you work through the day then that is it. I did spend an awful lot of time thinking about projects and working for people outside normal working hours. I think you can only do that when you are older, when you have had all the fun and frolics and bright lights and running around and love and marriage and all that.

A high proportion (37%) of spouses were self-employed (Table 8.7), although in eight of the 15 cases, husbands had become full-time business partners in their wife's firm after a successful start-up. The reasons for husbands entering the business varied: some businesses provided improved career prospects for husbands; in others women needed managerial assistance but were reluctant to employ an unknown manager outside the family; occasionally, husbands were needed to act as financial guarantors for recurrent finance. The effect of husbands joining the business tended to be extreme. For four of the women who had asked partners to join the business, their moral support and business guidance was welcomed. But for other women, the effect was catastrophic for their confidence and credibility. They interpreted it as a sign of personal failure and felt removed from their previous position of manager and proprietor.

Table 8.7 Occupation of husband or domestic partner ($n = 40$).

	No.
Self-employed	
Business partner	8
Own business	7
Employee	
Managerial	6
Other professional	13
Public sector	2
Sales	2
Manual	2
Total	40

One woman, the owner of a Nottingham-based clothes manufacturing firm, asked her husband to join her firm as a co-director with the intention that they could co-manage the businesses. Her husband resigned his position of manager in another firm and within a short period had taken over tasks such as financial management, book-keeping, employee supervision and marketing, relegating her to the status of designer. The additional pressure of the family's entire income being directly linked to the success of the firm was an unwelcome burden.

> I am bitterly disappointed about the whole thing, okay the business is very successful and the people are nice; only this morning I had a buyer on the phone complimenting me on the lines and ordering fifty dozen more for next year. But that doesn't make up for the way I feel now, I should never have started it, and I should never have asked Paul to come in. It's been awful.

Another woman commented:

> I should have known better—after all these years of seeing him around the house.

Relationships With Children

A large majority of respondents stated that business ownership improved their relations with their children. Only five respondents felt that proprietorship had a detrimental effect upon their relationship with their children (Table 8.6). The reasons given for this included the flexibility of their working hours, involvement of the children in the business and the proprietor's own greater self-assurance. Women who had been in business longer were most positive, reflecting the facts that their children were older and the relationships and routines of combining business and domestic life were more established. Some women felt that business ownership had a positive 'role model' effect upon their children, especially daughters, and many hoped that their daughters would follow them into business ownership.

Although it is clear that for many women proprietorship served to improve the quality of their relationship with their children, the burden of responsibility for both business and domestic commitments proved costly. The tension which many working women feel between domestic and work commitments is well documented. For self-employed women, however, the time and energy required for business ownership increases this strain. One respondent described how she felt:

We can't go on like this forever, I think that we will eventually end up making ourselves ill. We snatched a week's holiday this summer—it was between the receptionist's holidays, but we had to be back in time to do the wages for the next week. That is all we got and I'm desperately aware that when somebody wants to discuss their homework problems I'm shattered... it's just that constant feeling that you can't do any aspect very well because you are pulled in so many directions.

Extensive use of good quality childcare provision was the most common practical response to this problem. All of the respondents with children relied on either family support, or in most cases, paid help. Twenty of the sample (representing 71% of mothers) had encountered problems with childcare provision and domestic arrangements. The most commonly cited reasons were first, that reliable paid support was scarce and second, that when it was available, it was expensive and ineligible for tax relief.

Generally, where childcare was brought in, the female interviewee was responsible for both its organization and payment. Even where male partners were in full-time employment or self-employment, childcare was seen as a cost to be borne by the woman.

Responses to business ownership and motherhood varied between those running businesses on a part-time and full-time basis. The respondents whose businesses were most overtly affected by childcare commitments were those run on a part-time basis or those trading from home. These respondents had addressed the needs of their children, and their personal need to spend time with them, by organizing their businesses around them.

When Alex is due to be collected then I like to make sure that I am there to collect him. Weekends I hope to get sorted out when Alex goes to play-group, I'll then, hopefully, be able to turn my weekend working into the week working ... I found that you really have got to concentrate so much of your efforts into the time that you have got to work. You can't let it drift over to the next day because perhaps you can't afford to work the next day, because you haven't got a child minder. You have constantly got to keep on top of things just in case you're not available for work.

Now that I am working completely for myself I have structured it, since I sold the part of the business that was dealing with retail and now that I am dealing only with mail order, now I can fit the children in. So, if I have to leave at three to pick up the children from school, it's no problem. I can take my work home with me. Whatever needs to be done, I can do it at home.

Another respondent set up a small advertising consultancy when she became aware that she could not sustain the antisocial hours worked by her male colleagues, have children, and still pursue her career. As she said:

> I just want to be able to sit down and write when I want to, and go out shopping when I want to. If I would rather spend the day out in the park with the children and work at night, I can.

Of the respondents who were dividing their working week between their businesses and their children, the two whose companies have maintained a rapid rate of growth both relied on co-directors to sustain the impetus for growth. It seems that, unless women business owners have developed a substantial support network for their business, enabling them to withdraw from full-time working, it is unlikely that their businesses will be growth orientated in the short term.

The parents who operated their businesses on a full-time basis often had to learn to delegate tasks at an earlier stage than would be the case for most men. A large proportion of the 28 women in the sample who had children were paying for childcare or domestic help. In the words of one woman:

> You should be expounding all your energy on what you are good at. You should be able to earn enough money to pay somebody to do it better than you can do it . . . Whether it's baking scones, washing socks or typing letters. You should recognize that and set it aside on an appropriate budget. Then you should be able to do what you are good at and do it even better. It should have a knock-on effect.

Initial feelings of guilt at not fulfilling traditional female roles were common, although generally a working compromise between home and business was soon reached.

> I'm trying to make changes, which will alleviate me having to sacrifice family life, because I often work at home in the evenings, and I've got my little boy, where I feel I should be spending some time with him. I hate to keep saying "mummy's working".

> The washing basket is full. The fridge is empty. What happens is that you move near to a Safeway store that is open from eight o'clock in the morning until eight o'clock at night, seven days a week.

For many female entrepreneurs, therefore, the learning process in delegating tasks begins in the early stages of their business career. However, many women who had been in demanding jobs, working inconsistent hours, before entering self-employment, had often made decisions about childcare before becoming self-employed. Among our sample it appears that the traditional male/female roles are adhered to in relationships between parents and children, and between the female business owner and her domestic partner. Where the women interviewed did not perceive themselves to be fulfilling traditional maternal and conjugal roles, feelings of stress and guilt were common.

Quality of Life

The study provides interesting insights into the effects of business ownership upon the quality of life. Relationships with friends, social life, time for self, health, income, and perceptions of quality of life were among the issues explored with respondents.

Relationships with friends were often seen to have deteriorated (Table 8.6). Lack of time was viewed as a more important factor in this rather than business ownership *per se*. It is possible that as more women enter self-employment and business ownership as a long term career, there will be a greater 'normalization' of entrepreneurship and consequently greater scope for maintaining and developing social and personal relationships with these time constraints.

> As it is, one of the things I find quite difficult is that I don't have a lot of free time. I find it extremely difficult to meet my friends and we have to make specific arrangements and make sure that you get that time, because it would be very difficult if you lost it.

For many women the ensuing job satisfaction of proprietorship outweighed detrimental effects upon social life. Where these areas had improved it tended to be where the respondent had developed friends through the business, or where the business had come to provide a social life. Among young women this was often a deliberate strategy. As one explained:

> I have a completely different circle of friends now. All my friends are professional women, although not necessarily self-employed ones. All my friends now, are very career minded, mostly still single. My social life has just completely changed, because I now do a lot of water sports, just for relaxation. There is more need to unwind and relax and forget about your work. None of us can sit down and do nothing for long.

The combination of business networks and social activity was common, suggesting that women's clubs or other similar mechanisms may have an important role to play in future responses to the pressure for women's enterprise networks.

Table 8.8 Has going into business on your own improved or deteriorated your:

	Income No.	Social life No.	Other family relationships No.
Better	27	16	20
Worse	26	26	12
No difference	5	18	21
Don't know	2	0	0
Not applicable	0	0	7
Total	60	60	60

Income was most affected by business ownership, although respondents were evenly split between whether this effect has been positive or negative (Table 8.8). It would seem reasonable that income would suffer most during the start-up phase, as sustained low income would drive many small business owners out of self-employment, while successful start-up would produce higher returns over time.

Although half the sample felt that their health was unaffected by business ownership, almost one third believed that they were less healthy (Table 8.9). Stress-related ailments were frequently mentioned. Although health self-assessment is generally considered to be unreliable, other women noted an improvement in their health, largely because they were too busy to admit to or recognize commonplace ailments such as coughs and colds.

Table 8.9 Has going into business on your own improved or deteriorated your:

	Health No.	Family health No.	Time for yourself No.	Quality of life No.
Better	9	4	10	42
Worse	19	0	37	10
No difference	32	45	11	6
Don't know	0	0	2	2
Not applicable	0	11	0	0
Total	60	60	60	60

In one extreme case, during start-up, a respondent took only 1 day off work after undergoing a mastectomy as treatment for breast cancer. Although she attributed her cancer to the stress of starting up and the extraordinary pressure to succeed, she linked her subsequent recuperation with the desire to keep close to her business.

Despite many of the disappointments recorded by the women when questioned about family relationships and other factors which may have been adversely affected by business ownership, a large majority stated that the general quality of their life had been improved by starting in business (Table 8.9). Lack of time and occasionally insufficient income were the reasons most commonly given for any deterioration in quality of life. For most, self-employment had actively improved their lives:

> Self-employment has given me a lot of experience which I wouldn't have had . . . a lot of satisfaction and a lot of reward.

Table 8.10   Satisfaction with lifestyle factors.

How do you feel about:	Satisfaction (1 = very satisfied: 7 = very unsatisfied)						
	1	2	3	4	5	6	7
Yourself: what you are accomplishing and the way you handle problems	5	24	20	7	3	1	0
Your family life: husband, marriage and children	9	14	16	8	6	2	1
The income you and your family have	5	9	16	8	7	10	4
The amount of fun and enjoyment you have	10	15	15	7	6	3	3
Your house or home	23	12	10	5	4	3	3
The things you and your family do	2	10	7	15	11	9	6
The way you spend your spare time or non-working activities	6	18	15	5	7	5	4
Your health and general condition	10	21	14	6	4	4	1
Your business	8	22	17	7	5	0	1

As a final report on their relative satisfaction with their current lives, respondents were asked to rank a number of statements dealing with lifestyle factors. The results, reported in Table 8.10, confirm that dissatisfaction was most noticeable when ranking leisure activities for themselves and their families and their relative income. The majority of women were especially satisfied with two particular elements of their lives: their business and their accomplishments.

CASE STUDY

Company activity: *Textile Design and Manufacture*
Company started: *January 1986*
Employees: *2*
Business organization: *Sole Trader*

Company History

This respondent designs and prints fabrics, as well as manufacturing various scarves and fabrics. She sells her produce wholesale. The business is relatively young and can only justify two employees though the respondent hopes to increase this number. Both employees are female, one helps with the manufacturing while the other assists with administration. This respondent has clear objectives for her business which reflect her purposeful attitude to life. After graduating in textile design she applied for several vacancies and was refused as she was thought to be too talented to work for someone else. Soon after, she was approached by Liberty for some designs and given 6 months to start up a business and service the order.

As a finalist in last year's Livewire competition, she has successfully applied to the Princes Trust for funding. After servicing the initial orders, she has now widened her customer base to include several major department stores. Currently she is in the process of moving to larger premises.

Start Up

The business was started with £10 000 which was made up of a bank loan (40%), a mortgage (20%), local enterprise agency (10%), and a local authority grant (30%). The capital was invested in machinery and a certain amount of stock. Some problems were experienced with the Local Authority grant. The money would only be released after the bank loan was secured. The respondent had nothing more to offer as security and was forced to turn to her family for help. They were able to deposit the equivalent of the bank loan. The business started trading from a serviced office which she rents from the local authority. They helped her find the premises. The biggest problems faced by this respondent were caused by insufficient start up capital. She feels that the business was unnecessarily handicapped in the first year.

Barriers and Strategies for Success

Access to regular finance from institutional sources had been a problem for this respondent. However the major problem she is currently facing is staffing the business to cope with contracts without incurring prohibitive labour costs. Support from family and friends is temporarily alleviating this problem. She talked a great deal of the importance of her family:

> The family I believe is one of the most important things you can have. Because there have been times, when I have had to work say, 7 days—we didn't go home at all, we worked 24 hours. My mother would come here, she doesn't mind leaving her job to stay with me all night, to meet the particular order. My sisters, as you can see, will come here and work, and the family has been the most important thing in my business so far. You can't do it all by yourself.

9

Conclusions: Developing the Future for Women in Business

The aim of this book has been to describe the reasons why women start in business; their experiences of business ownership; their problems, both gender and non-gender related; and, most importantly, the strategies they develop for overcoming barriers. The way women approach starting an enterprise is dominated by the stage they have reached in their life cycle, that is, their age and their domestic relationships. Differentiation by personal life cycle is important as women start businesses at very different points in their lives. This affects the types of businesses started and their individual approach to business ownership. From the analysis of motivations and experiences at start-up, five broad groups of women emerged.

The majority of the women interviewed were highly motivated towards achievement and were represented within either the younger, achievement-orientated group, the aspirants, or within the high achiever group of older women who had often come out of successful careers to start a business. Personal and career-related experience and attitudes towards business ownership, which formed the initial basis for group classification, also had an impact on the type of firm started and determined the style of management utilized by the entrepreneur. The achievement-orientated groups tended towards non-traditional sectors, such as construction, engineering and manufacturing, as well as constituting the majority of proprietors within the new sectors, such as business services and new technology-based industries.

A smaller number of women had drifted into business ownership from less relevant backgrounds, often being unemployed before start-up. The accidentalists were also characterized by their relative youthfulness. Their approach to business demonstrated their marginal attachment to self-employment. Negative experiences of business ownership could deter them from continuing. Positive experiences had the opposite effect of making them more determined to succeed in business. Businesses started by accidentalists tended to be in sectors where barriers to entry, in terms of finance and technical knowledge, were perceived to be low.

The traditionalists had a family history of self-employment. For this group, self-employment and business ownership was the norm, employment the exception. Unlike the achievement-orientated groups, the traditionalists did not have high expectations in terms of success and growth of the firm. The traditionalists saw self-employment as a means of earning a comfortable, if relatively modest, living. They were more likely to reach a 'comfort level' of prosperity, beyond which they were unprepared to strive for further success.

The final group, re-entrants, represent a common phenomena in contemporary Britain. Women with children now tend to have a more continuous working life, with spells of paid work between children and an earlier return to work after the youngest child reaches school age. Women now spend more of their potential working lives in employment and the trend is towards increasing participation. The past 20 years have also seen an increase in women's expectations of personal fulfilment on a number of different fronts. These include employment, earnings levels, and the ability to combine careers with motherhood. This enthusiasm notwithstanding, a continuing and significant level of unemployment has proved to be a substantial obstacle to the realization of these expectations. Women wishing to return to remunerative employment are choosing business ownership as a means of fulfilling their aspirations. In this study, the re-entrants represent women who return to economic activity after motherhood and who choose self-employment. This activity allows them to participate economically, but on their own terms. For many women in this group, self-employment was initially a part-time activity. Businesses were deliberately restricted to a small scale until the owners could devote more time to them. Starting on a part-time basis was not seen to have any effect on the ultimate size or prosperity of the business.

The lives and career histories of women entrepreneurs vary considerably. Most of the women identified in this study had undertaken some kind of further education, varying from vocational courses such as secretarial studies to, in one case, a doctorate in business administration. This contrasts markedly with findings about male entrepreneurs and owner-managers. The successful women in this study proved to be better educated than either the failed business owners in the parallel study or the total population of women (cf. the 1987 analysis of the General Household Survey undertaken by Curran *et al.*). The career paths pursued by the women interviewed were usually in traditionally female employment sectors, such as retailing and within service industries. Only a minority had participated in non-traditional sectors before starting in business. There were instances where women had spent their careers working in traditionally female occupations, such as textile machining, and had started businesses within the same sector as manufacturers. The successful female entrepreneurs were more likely to start businesses in an industry in which they had direct experience than the unsuccessful women business owners.

Regardless of their educational and career backgrounds, all had experienced problems in starting and running enterprises. Many of these were operational problems which affect male business owners as well as women. Many of the women who participated in this study believed that even operational problems common to both male and female owners had a hidden gender dimension which exacerbated their effect on women-owned businesses. Other problems were seen as being specifically related to the gender of the business owner. The way the respondents approached these obstacles differed. There were, however, broad similarities in the strategies they adopted for dealing with problems. Deliberate policies of training, professionalization and networking were commonly adopted by the successful women.

Young women lacking in management experience adopted a deliberate strategy of training for business ownership to compensate for their youth and lack of relevant business and career experience. The view that it is the lack of prior experience which differentiates women and men in business was common among the respondents. For young women, without the benefit of either prior management or often work experience, this situation is exacerbated. Many reacted by consciously developing a strategy of training which enabled them to compensate for youth as well as gender.

Older women tended towards a strategy of professionalization to overcome gender-related problems, sublimating their gender and personal position to gain external credibility and confidence. This approach was strongly associated with market success especially in the early periods of business ownership. The two frequently identified situations in which this approach was used were raising finance and competing for orders. Conversely, several women thought that they were at an advantage over male business owners. Many respondents were willing to exploit their femininity in group situations or in certain types of negotiation, turning the perceived disadvantages of gender into an advantage.

Networking, as a strategy to compensate for gender, was frequently used by the successful women. Not only was networking used as a management strategy, it was also used as a start-up mechanism which helped in advice gathering and the market research process. Networking was also used, particularly by women operating in non-traditional sectors, as a means of establishing themselves in industries. It also helped women to redress the isolation of business ownership. Established business owners recognized the need for networking as a tool to help other women in business. Consequently, many women acted as role models and mentors for other women starting in business.

The development of management styles tended to be closely linked to the management strategies developed by individual respondents. Strategies were often developed to cope with and counteract gender-related difficulties. While Goffee and Scase (1985) interpret business ownership in itself as a strategy to overcome female subordination in the labour market, a proposition supported here, further evidence from this study suggests that women confront gender-related barriers within proprietorship. Management strategies were used to overcome these barriers. Strategies were either deliberately adopted or evolved incrementally as businesses became more sophisticated. In the majority of cases, success was seen as being attributable to these strategies.

The parallel study of women whose businesses had ceased trading highlighted contrasting experience. These women tended to lack educational achievement and relevant career backgrounds. Among this group, precipitous and unprepared market entry was common. Although the employment generated by these firms was comparatively high, 87 of the 94 jobs created were within three firms. The owners of companies which had failed did not develop strategies to overcome obstacles, neither did they recognize the need for strategic management until after the demise of their firms.

It is clear from this study that, not only are women entering proprietorship in increasing numbers, but that they do so in the face of many tangible and intangible obstacles. Despite these barriers they demonstrate a strong determination to succeed. Their contribution in bringing prosperity to themselves, their families and to the economy in general has been largely unrecognized until recent years. While many significant government and local initiatives have been introduced with the intention of stimulating entrepreneurship and improving the climate for small business start-up, few have taken into account the differing barriers faced by women who wish to start in business.

It is a conclusion of this study that policies designed to assist individuals start a business need to be re-evaluated to ensure the inclusion of female experience of business ownership. There has been a proliferation of initiatives designed to assist small business owners. These have ranged from the provision of professional advice for start-up by training and enterprise companies in England and Wales and the equivalent Local Enterprise Council's in Scotland, to financial measures such as the Enterprise Allowance Scheme, the Loan Guarantee Scheme and Business Expansion Scheme. Other forms of help have included the provision of specially designed industrial property and managed workspaces for small businesses. The experiences of the women interviewed in this study were that few of these initiatives were relevant or targeted to their specific needs.

The past 3 years have seen the introduction of some locally based programmes of assistance for women intending to start in business. Their introduction has, so far, been dependent on interested and influential activists and their coverage has been piecemeal. Successful schemes of assistance for women have included locally based venture capital funds for women intending to start up, single sex small business training programmes for women, and an increase in the number of female counsellors in small business advisory agencies. None of these schemes of assistance can, single-handedly, combat the structural influences which affect women. National programmes designed for women, which are integrated within existing small business advisory services, may prove to be more appropriate.

Ultimately, however, female entrepreneurship must be recognized for what it is. Nationally it has great importance for future economic prosperity. Individually, business ownership provides women with the independence they crave and with economic and social satisfaction. For many women, therefore, entrepreneurship is a liberating experience.

Appendix

Research Methodology and Sample Profile

This study starts from a position where underlying issues are not always clear, and where a representative sample is difficult to devise. To overcome these difficulties the research team initially adopted a case study approach, focusing primarily upon qualitative rather than quantitative data. It was envisaged that a small amount of statistical data would be collected mainly for the purposes of classifying the sample. The main issues, however, were to be elicited by non-directive questioning. During the early stages of the project there was a change in emphasis from a mostly unstructured qualitative approach to one where the main information was gathered using a structured questionnaire complemented by open-ended questions and some unstructured interview themes. Constraints imposed by the relatively short time scale involved were important reasons for the shift in emphasis. There was little time to develop and pilot techniques to minimize interobserver subjectivity and bias during interviews. There was insufficient time too for the researchers to gain some insight and appreciation of each others' idiosyncrasies, and the effect these might have upon comparative data.

Using a questionnaire containing set questions complemented with open-ended and non-directive questions, the research team was able to collect both types of data for analysis. Structured elements of the questionnaire enabled us to maintain comparability across interviewers for the purposes of analysis; open-ended questions allowed the researchers an insight into the lives of the participants.

The bulk of the fieldwork was undertaken in two rounds of personal interviews with the 70 respondents. The first interviews, conducted between July and August 1987, lasted between 2 and $4\frac{1}{2}$ hours. An in-depth, semi-structured questionnaire was used to elicit quantitative data with a minimal standard of comparability across interviewers. Much of the quantitative data was coded and computer analysed (SPSS-X) and tabulated. Open-ended and non-directive questions, forming the bulk of the qualitative data, were taped and later transcribed for analysis.

Follow-up, fully taped interviews conducted between October and December 1987 were intended to fill gaps not covered in the first round and to explore more carefully issues of management style and growth. Unlike the first interviews, the follow-up was mostly unstructured and conducted around a series of points outlined on a checklist. The short time span between interviews did not allow for diachronic analysis. Surprisingly, however, significant changes had taken place in many companies even within this short period.

For many participants, the interviews were the first time that they had been given an opportunity to talk about their professional and personal ambitions. For some, the discussion clarified thoughts about the business and the way that it was run. It cannot be discounted that the interview itself may have affected the future of the business. The second round of interviews confirmed this impression; many women stated that they had received either a boost or a jolt from our intervention.

There are problems inherent in relying upon verbal reports and individual experience to investigate gender-related issues as the social and political backgrounds of the interviewees determine to an extent whether discrimination is perceived and recognized as such. Many interviewees stated that they were not feminists and, moreover, appeared hostile to that philosophy. As one interviewee said:

> I'm not a women's libber or anything like that and I don't get on my high horse about it. I'm just doing my job like anybody else. I just happen to be a woman.

The interview itself, therefore, may be a determining factor as the interviewer, by probing and encouraging the interviewee to discuss her experiences in terms of gender, may raise the level of consciousness and recognition of gender discrimination among the sample. A number of respondents could not identify any single area where, as women, they had been at a disadvantage, but felt that generally business ownership is more difficult for women.

Sample Collection

The lack of an appropriate data source of female business owners makes sampling difficult in this field of research. As such, a number of sources were used to locate the respondents. Local enterprise agencies (LEAs), training organizations, district councils and the Shell (UK) Ltd-sponsored Livewire competition provided the majority of names and addresses used in this sample. Universities, polytechnics and colleges of further education known to run small business courses within the three research areas were contacted and many co-operated by providing names and addresses of female former participants on business start-up and development courses. A variety of other methods of locating possible respondents were used, including articles in local newspapers, contacting employers and business organizations, and by following up informal sources throughout the investigation. Inevitably, a reliance upon small firms advisory and training organizations may have had a distorting effect upon the sample in some aspects, for example, in their educational backgrounds and attitudes to training.

Despite the problems inherent in its construction, an appropriate sample emerged through the use of a wide variety of both formal and informal sources and with the co-operation of almost every woman approached. This allowed the researchers to collect enough data to structure the sample along the necessary dimensions.

The sample was organized to reflect a diversity of industrial and business situations. As a consequence, the sample is not representative of female business ownership. Rather, it was selected to illustrate a variety of ways women participate in business. Selection enabled the researchers to control the inclusion of businesses that could illustrate the key areas of interest. The final sample displays the heterogeneity of female business ownership.

The main sample of 50 ongoing businesses was originally expanded to include two outriding samples of 10 women who were in the process of starting up in business and 10 women who had ceased trading. The inclusion of two additional groups allowed the researchers to provide a fuller picture of contemporary female entrepreneurship from pre-start-up to business expansion. During the first round of interviews it became apparent that isolating the new start subsample would prove problematic. Many of the self-selecting pre-starts had, in fact, developed further both in firm size and market share than some companies in the main sample. As a consequence, this subsample was merged with the main sample to provide 60 case studies of ongoing firms. To differentiate newer businesses from the more established, cross-sectional analysis by firm age (less than 1 year, 1–5 years, over 5 years) was undertaken. Eighteen firms in the main sample had been established for less than 1 year. The sample of 10 businesses which had ceased trading remained, and the results of this subsample are described in Chapter 7.

Sample Profile

The sample of 60 business case studies was rigorously structured along the following dimensions: industrial sector; life cycle; business organization; and geographical location. The additional 'outriding' sample of 10 businesses which had ceased trading expanded the total sample to 70 case studies. While the final sample did not constitute an exact matrix, the businesses were broadly divided by the various dimensions.

Industrial Sector

Three kinds of industrial sector were identified as being of interest in this study: non-traditional; traditional; and new. Non-traditional sectors have been defined as those where women constitute a minority of those employed in the industry, examples being heavy engineering, construction and manufacturing. Traditional sectors, conversely, are those where the majority of employees are female, such as office services, retail and distribution. Companies in the new sectors (usually new technology or service-based) operate across a variety of areas growing in importance in terms of employment and contribution to GNP.

Table A.1 compares the sample businesses with the self-employed population of women as a whole, and illustrates the skew in the sample

Table A.1   Respondents by industrial sector.

Sector	No. in sample	%	Self-employed (females) in Great Britain ($\times 10^3$)	%
Agriculture	2	3	28	4.0
Chemicals manufacturing	4	6	3	*
Metals manufacturing	1	1	7	1.0
Other manufacturing	19	27	41	5.9
Construction	1	1	19	2.7
Retail/distribution/hotel and catering	16	23	280	40.3
Banking/financial services	15	21	69	9.9
Other services	12	17	247	35.6
Total	70	100	694	100

* Less than 0.5%.
Source: Labour Force Survey, 1987.

towards businesses in the 'other manufacturing' and 'banking and financial services' sectors and away from 'retail, distribution, hotel and catering', and 'other services' sectors. This not only reflects the researchers' concentration on women in non-traditional sectors, but also the largely traditional patterns of business activity present in the three geographical areas. Companies in the Nottingham area were dominated by those in the 'other manufacturing' (clothing) sector, whereas financial services and service-based companies were predominant in London. 'Construction', 'chemicals manufacturing' and 'metals manufacturing' were represented in Glasgow. Overall, however, the sample businesses are spread more evenly over a variety of sectors than is the case for the total population of female employers and self-employed.

Life Cycle

Stratification by age produced a sample more closely related to that of the total population of female business owners (Table A.2). A comparison with results of the General Household Survey (GHS) (Curran *et al.*, 1987) shows a similar proportion of women within the medial age ranges, but with a skew in the present sample towards young women and away from the older age ranges. Different age ranges ensured that the sample included women at a variety of stages in their lives. Deliberately included in the study were women who had moved into enterprise from economic inactivity, older women without children and young women with little experience of employment.

Table A.2   Respondents by age.

Age of respondent	No. in sample	% in sample	GHS female sample (%)*
16–25	13	19	1.8
26–40	37	53	75.5
41–55	18	26	†
Over 55	2	3	22.8
Total	70	100‡	

* Based on female small business owners.
† Due to inconsistencies with age ranges, three age ranges of the General Household Survey (26–55) have been rounded up to produce an aggregate figure.
‡ Rounded.

The marital status of the sample also differed in some ways from GHS results. A large proportion of the sample were either married (27) or in a stable relationship (13). Of the remaining 20 in the main sample, 12 were single, six divorced, one separated and one widowed. While results from the GHS also report a high number of married women (75.4%), differences do occur in the other groups. In particular, there is a significantly higher occurrence of single and divorced women and fewer widows than in the GHS results. Similar studies undertaken in this area have also noted a higher incidence of divorcees than found in the GHS study (cf. Watkins and Watkins, 1984; Goffee and Scase, 1985). While Curran (1986) associates this apparent anomaly with non-random sampling techniques, the now frequently found incidence of divorcees in independent studies (with no deliberate skew of marital status) makes this a point worth exploring.

Business Age and Organization

The age of the companies in the sample varied between less than 1 year (18) and 23 years, although the majority had been trading for 2 years. While a variety of organizational structures were represented, sole traders and partnerships were especially common among the younger businesses; limited companies were favoured by the older, more established enterprises (Table A.3). Ten of the partnerships were run in conjunction with other women (usually in similar situations/life cycle). Of the eight run in conjunction with men, these were either husbands or domestic partners, usually brought into the business after a successful female start-up period. Reasons for them entering the business are explored in Chapter 5.

Sample stratification and a dependence upon mainstream and non-traditional businesses has probably led to a slight distortion in the types of

Table A.3 Business organization.

Business organization	No. in sample	%
Sole trader	22	37
Partnership	18	30
Limited company	17	28
Co-operative	2	3
Franchise	1	2
Total	60	100

business organization included in the study. While the research team was aware of a number of women-only collectives and community-based businesses, mostly in London, these were limited to two co-operatives in this study.

Ethnicity

Ethnicity was not a determining factor in sample stratification. Three participants (4%) were of Afro-Caribbean origin: two sole traders and one partnership. No Asian-owned firms were included in the study. Comparisons with the GHS reveal that this is a higher figure than for the female self-employed average, but lower than for female small business owners. The role of the 'ethnic factor' (Wilson, 1987) was perceived by these respondents as presenting them with further burdens in addition to gender-related problems.

Educational Background and Employment Experience

The educational background of the sample was generally exceptionally high. The respondents' ages at leaving school suggest a strong motivation towards achievement even at the early stages of their careers, with 42% leaving at 18. Only nine of the 60 attained no qualifications. Of the rest 34 obtained A levels or the equivalent.

The personal emphasis placed on education and training among the sample is reflected in the number who went into further education. No less than 57 women took part in full-time or part-time further education. Of these all obtained at least one qualification; 24 graduated with a degree, 17 achieved HND/HNC non-graduate teaching or nursing qualifications, and seven received a qualification in business training. A few women interviewed, notably those operating within the new sectors, had either undertaken or were in the process of undertaking a postgraduate degree at either Masters or Doctoral level.

Sampling techniques and an emphasis upon non-traditional and new sectors are probably responsible for this bias towards education and training. A comparison with the GHS data shows just how distinctive this bias is. Only 11% of female and 8.6% of male small business owners surveyed in the GHS reported any further education qualifications, compared with 81% within the present study.

Previous work experience indicates that a majority of the sample were highly motivated towards a career of some kind and most had spent a

large proportion of their lives at work. In addition, most had an exceptionally positive attitude towards working, although not necessarily employment. Fifty per cent held between two and four previous jobs and 35%
more than five jobs prior to start-up. Employment immediately prior to
business start-up varied considerably: 20 held either managerial or
professional posts; five secretarial or clerical; four were in sales; one
manual; four were housewives; and 14 unemployed. Eight of the sample
were already self-employed before starting their present enterprise.

A high proportion of the sample (78%) had some family connection
with self-employment during their lifetime. Forty-one per cent of the
sample had husbands or domestic partners who were self-employed, and
13 came from families where either their mother or father were self-
employed. Of the total number of small businesses connected to the
respondents, 42 were described as being very successful, 20 as moderately successful and only 13 described as not successful.

References and Bibliography

Allen, S. and Truman, C. (1988) Women's work and success in women's businesses. Paper presented to the 11th UK National Small Firms Policy and Research Conference.

Amsden, A. H. (ed.) (1980) *The Economics of Women and Work*. Penguin, Middlesex.

Ansoff, I. (1987) *Corporate Strategy*. Penguin, Harmondsworth.

Barron, K. D. and Norris, G. M. (1976) Sexual divisions and the dual labour market. In: Barker, D. and Allen, S. (eds) *Dependence and Exploitation in Work and Marriage*. Longman, London.

Begley, T. M. and Boyd, D. P. (1987) Psychological characteristics associated with performance in entrepreneurial firms and smaller businesses. *Journal of Business Venturing* **2(1)**, 79–93

Bennett, E. M. and Cohen, L. R. (1959) Men and women: personality patterns and contrasts. *Genetic Psychology Monographs* **59**, 101–155.

Bierhoff-Alfermann, D. (1977) *Psychologie der Geschlechtsunterschiede*. Kiepenheuer und Witsch, Koln.

Bruegel, I. (1982) Women as a reserve army of labour: a note on recent British experience. In: Evans, M. (ed.), *The Woman Question*. Fontana, London.

Cannon, T. (1987) The way ahead. Paper presented to the 1987 Enterprise Convention, LEDU, Northern Ireland.

Cannon, T., Carter, S., Faulkner, W. and Nenadic, S. (1989) The nature, the role and the impact of small business research. In: Rosa, P. *et al.* (eds), *The Role and Contribution of Small Business Research*. Gower, Aldershot.

Carsrud, A. L. (1988) The psychology of entrepreneurship. Teaching Module 5.6., University of Stirling, Scotland.

Carter, S. and Cannon, T. (1988a) Women in business. *Employment Gazette*, October, pp. 565–571.

Carter, S. and Cannon, T. (1988b) Female entrepreneurs: a study of female business owners; their motivations, experiences and strategies for success. Department of Employment Research Paper No. 65, November.

Casson, M. (1982) *The Entrepreneur: An Economic Theory*. Martin Robinson, Oxford.

Central Statistical Office (1988) *Regional Trends 23*. HMSO, London.

Chiplin, B. and Sloane, P. J. (1974) Sexual discrimination in the labour market. *British Journal of Industrial Relations*, November.

Chiplin, B. and Sloane, P. J. (1982) *Tackling Discrimination at the Work Place: An Analysis of Sex Discrimination in Britain*. Cambridge University Press, Cambridge.

Collom, D. (1981) *Canadian Women Owner Managers*. Ottowa Small Business Secretariat, Ottowa.

Coyle, A. (1982) Sex and skill in the organization of the clothing industry. In: West, J. (ed.), *Work, Women and the Labour Market*. Routledge Kegan Paul, London.

Coyle, A. (1984) *Redundant Women*. The Women's Press, London.

Creigh, S. (1986) Self-employment in Britain: results from the Labour Force Surveys 1981–1984. *Employment Gazette*, May, pp. 183–194.

Cromie, S. (1987) Similarities and differences between women and men who choose business proprietorship. *International Small Business Journal* **5** (3), 43–60.

Cromie, S. and Hayes, J. (1988) Towards a typology of female entrepreneurs. *The Sociological Review* **36(1)**, February.

Curran, J. (1986) *Bolton Fifteen Years On: A Review and Analysis of Small Business Research in Britain 1971–1986*. Small Business Research Trust, London.

Curran, J., Stanworth, J. and Watkins, D. (eds) (1986) *The Survival of the Small Firm*, Vols 1–2. Gower, Aldershot.

Curran, J., Burrows, R. and Evandrou, M. (1987) *Small Business Owners and the Self Employed in Britain: A Secondary Analysis of General Household Survey Data*. Small Business Research Trust, London.

Deaux, K. (1976) Sex: a perspective on the attribution process. In: Harvey, J. H. *et al*. (eds), *New Directions in Attribution Research*, Vol.1. Hillsdale, New Jersey.

Department of Employment (1988) 1987 Labour Force Survey—preliminary results. *Employment Gazette* March, pp. 144–158.

Dex, S. (1987) *Women's Occupational Mobility*. Macmillan, London.

Equal Opportunities Commission (1989) *Women and Men in Britain 1989*. HMSO, London.

Evans, M. (ed.) (1982) *The Woman Question: Readings on the Subordination of Women*. Fontana, London.

Foley, P. and Green, H. (1989) *Small Business Success*. Paul Chapman Publishing for the Small Business Research Trust, London.

Fothergill, S. and Gudgin, G. (1982) *Unequal Growth: Urban and Regional Employment Change in the UK*. Heinnemann, London.

Ganguly, P. and Bannock, G. (1985) *UK Small Business Statistics and International Comparisons*. Harper and Row/Small Business Research Trust, London.

Gibb, A. A. and Ritchie, J. (1981) Influences in entrepreneurship: a study over time. Paper presented to the 1981 Small Business Policy and Research Conference, 20–21 November, Polytechnic of Central London.

Gibb, A. A. and Ritchie, J. (1982) Understanding the process of starting a small business. *European Small Business Journal* **1(1)**.

Goffee, R. and Scase, R. (1985) *Women in Charge: The Experiences of Female Entrepreneurs*. Allen and Unwin, London.

Goffee, R. and Scase, R. (1983) Business ownership and women's subordination: a preliminary study of female proprietors. *Sociological Review*, **31**, 624–648.

Goffee, R., Scase, R. and Pollack, M. (1982) Why some women decide to become their own boss. *New Society* 9 September, 408–410.

Hakim, C. (1979) Occupational segregation. Department of Employment Research Paper No. 9, London.

Hakim, C. (1981) Job segregation: trends in the 1970s. *Employment Gazette* December, pp. 521–529.

Hisrich, R. and Brush, C. (1983) The woman entrepreneur: implications of family, education and occupational experience. In: *Frontiers of Entrepreneurship Research Proceedings*. Babson College, Wellesley, MA, pp. 255–270.

Hisrich, R. and Brush, C. (1984) The woman entrepreneur. *Journal of Small Business Management* **22**(1), 30–37.

Hisrich, R. and Brush, C. (1986) *The Woman Entrepreneur*. Lexington Books, Lexington, MA.

Hymounts, C. (1986) The corporate women—the glass ceiling. *Wall Street Journal*.

Joshi H. E. (1984) Women's participation in paid work: further analysis of the women and employment survey. Department of Employment, Research Paper No. 45, HMSO, London.

Kets De Vries, M. F. R. (1977) The entrepreneurial personality: a person at the crossroads. *Journal of Management Studies*, **14**(1), 34–57.

Kimives, J. L. (1974) What are entrepreneurs made of? *Chemtech* December, 716–721.

Kirkham, J. (1987) Hidden assets: the use of domestic resources in a small business—a research note. Paper presented to the 10th National Small Firms Policy and Research Conference, Cranfield.

Kirzner, I. M. (1973) *Competition and Entrepreneurship*. University of Chicago Press, Chicago.

Lavoie, D. (1987) Today's women still face yesterday's values. *Small Business* **6**(3), 78–80.

Litvak, I. A. and Maule, C. J. (1974) Profiles of technical entrepreneurs. *Business Quarterly* **39**(2), 40–49.

London Business School (1983) *Small Business Bibliography*. London Business School, London.

Mancuso, J. R. (1984) What drives the entrepreneur? *Across The Board* **21**, 7–8, 43–47.

Marokjovic, M. (1987) *First European Survey of Women in Business*. EEC, Brussels.

Martin, J. and Roberts, C. (1984) *Women and Employment: A Lifetime Perspective*. The Report of the 1980 DE/OPCS Women and Employment Survey, HMSO, London.

Oakley, A. (1982) *Subject Women*. Fontana, London.

Potter, J. B. (1964) *Clinical Psychology*. Englewood Cliffs, NJ.

Report on the Committee of Inquiry on Small Firms (1971) HMSO, London.

Scase, R. and Goffee, R. (1980) *The Real World of the Small Business Owner*. Croom Helm, London.

Scase, R. and Goffee, R. (1982) *The Entrepreneurial Middle Class*. Croom Helm, London.

Schien, E. (1978) *Career Dynamics*. Addison Wesley, New York.

Schreier, J. (1975) *The Female Entrepreneur: A Pilot Study.* Centre for Venture Management, Milwaukee, WN.

Schumpeter, J. A. (1934) *The Theory of Economic Development.* Harvard University Press, Cambridge, MA.

Schumpeter, J. A. (1943) *Capitalism, Socialism and Democracy.* Allen and Unwin, London.

Schwartz, E. B. (1976) Entrepreneurship, a new female frontier. *Journal of Contemporary Business* **5**.

Scott, M. G. (1980) Independence and the flight from the large scale: some sociological factors in the founding process. In: Gibb, A. A. and Webb, T. (eds), *Policy Issues in Small Business Research.* Gower, Aldershot.

Small Business Research Trust (1990) *The NatWest Quarterly Survey of Small Business in Britain*, Vol. 6. No. 3.

Small Business Research Trust (1991) *The NatWest Quarterly Survey of Small Business in Britain*, Vol. 7. No. 1.

Solomon, G. T. and Fernald, L. W. (1988) Value profiles of male and female entrepreneurs. *International Small Business Journal* **6(3)**.

Stevenson, L. (1983) *An Investigation into the Entrepreneurial Experience of Women.* Vancouver UBC, ASAC Proceedings.

United States Small Business Administration (1985) *The State of Small Business 1985.* Washington.

Van der Wees, C. and Romijn, H. (1987) *Entrepreneurship and Small Enterprise Development For Women in Developing Countries: An Agenda of Unanswered Questions.* Management Development Programme, ILO, Geneva.

Veroff, J., McClelland, L. and Ruhland, D. (1975) Varieties of achievement motivation. In: Mednick, M. S. T. *et al.* (eds), *Women and Achievement.* Hemisphere, Washington.

Watkins, D. S. and Watkins, J. (1982) The female entrepreneur—American experience and its implications for the UK. In: Stanworth, J. *et al.* (eds), *Perspectives on a Decade of Small Business Research.* Gower, Aldershot.

Watkins, D. S. and Watkins, J. (1984) The female entrepreneur: her background and determinants of business choice, some British data. *International Small Business Journal* **2(4)**.

Watkins, J. M. and Watkins, D. S. (1986) The female entrepreneur: her background and determinants of business choice, some British data. In: Curran, J., Stanworth, J. and Watkins, D. (eds), *The Survival of the Small Firm.* Gower, Aldershot.

Weiner, B. (1972) *Theories of Motivation.* Markham, Chicago.

Weiner, M. (1981) *English Culture and the Decline of the Industrial Spirit 1850–1980.* Cambridge University Press, Cambridge.

West, J. (ed.) (1982) *Work, Women and the Labour Market.* Routledge and Kegan Paul, London.

Williams, S. (1985) *A Job To Live: The Impact of Tomorrow's Technology On Work and Society.* Penguin, London.

Wilson, P. (1987) *Growth Strategies in Minority Enterprises.* Small Business Research Trust, London.

Index